CONTAGIOUS DISEASES:

THEIR

HISTORY, ANATOMY, PATHOLOGY, AND TREATMENT.

WITH COMMENTS ON THE CONTAGIOUS DISEASES ACTS.

BY

WILLIAM MORGAN, M.D.,

*Member of the Royal College of Surgeons, England; Member of the British
Homœopathic Society; Physician to the Brighton Homœopathic Dispensary;
Formerly Physician to the North London Homœopathic Dispensary;
Accoucheur to the West End Maternity Institute; one of the
Medical Officers to the London Homœopathic
Hospital and the Cambridgeshire
Dispensary, &c., &c.*

FIRST EDITION.

LONDON:

JARROLD & SONS, 3, PATERNOSTER BUILDINGS;

THE HOMŒOPATHIC PUBLISHING COMPANY,
2, FINSBURY CIRCUS, E.C.;

BOERICKE & TAFEL, NEW YORK AND PHILADELPHIA.
And all Homœopathic Chemists and Booksellers.

1877.

CONTAGIOUS DISEASES.

WITH COMMENTS ON THE CONTAGIOUS DISEASES ACTS.

Dedit hanc contagio labem,
Et dabit in plures.

" Contagion has caused this plague spot, and will extend it to many more."—*Juvenal.*

PREFACE.

THE views propounded in the following pages, on the History, Anatomy, Pathology, and Treatment of "CONTAGIOUS DISEASES" were submitted in an abbreviated form to the consideration of the British Homœopathic Society at one of its meetings held some six years ago ; and although many of its members then present suggested its immediate publication, yet circumstances occurred which delayed its appearance in the form it is now presented to the reader till the present time.

Since then, however, the greater portion of the work has been re-written, and much practical matter has been added, which the author hopes may be found useful as well as interesting to those who may scan and consult its pages.

In undertaking the task of writing this work, the chief aim of the author has been to concentrate the largest amount of practical matter in the smallest possible compass; and whilst occasionally referring to a case of cure, in illustration of the action of a specifically chosen drug, he has, from a feeling of professional delicacy, avoided following the example of a recent writer on the same subject, by encumbering its scanty number of pages with a large number of claptrap sensational cases; resting content with the conviction that the practical bearing of the "Little Book" will be its best and most modest recommendation to public favour.

STAFFORD HOUSE, OLD STEINE, BRIGHTON:
 July 16th, 1877.

CONTENTS.

----&----

A 2

HOMŒOPATHIC MEDICINES.

Homœopathic Medicines.

THE homœopathic " Materia Medica" contains at
the present time from 260 to 270 medicinal preparations; the greater number of these have been faith-
fully proved on man, woman and child while in a
state of health, in order to ascertain the pathogenetic
and specific properties of each drug; others have
been but partially proved, and hold a place in its
pages on empirical grounds.

Homœopathic medicines are prepared and kept in
the form of Tinctures, Triturations, Pilules, and
Globules; a few in ether and glycerine, such as the
snake poisons.

The tinctures are chiefly derived from the vegetable
and animal kingdoms; known as expressed juice,
mother tincture, or matrix tincture, the symbol of
which is the Greek ϕ.

From these tinctures the various dilutions or

potencies are prepared ; and the higher we ascend in
the scale of dilution the further we depart from the
crude substance, which accounts for the non-poisonous
and consequently non-injurious properties of homœopathically prepared medicines ; but they nevertheless
retain medicinal properties of marvellous efficacy,
which are potent against the disease; and inert
against the constitution, when homœopathically or
specifically selected. Triturations, on the contrary,
are chiefly prepared from substances derived from the
mineral kingdom. Among these may be enumerated
sulphur, mercury, arsenic, zinc, tin, baryta, gold,
silver, iron, lime, copper, alum, tellurium, and many
more. The mode of preparing the various potencies,
from the matrix triturations is similar to those prepared from the tinctures, for the manipulation of
which the reader is referred to the pages of the
Homœopathic Pharmacopœia, recently published
under the auspices of the British Homœopathic
Society.

Pilules and Globules.

These little pellets, which have afforded our
allopathic brethren no scanty field for amusement and
ridicule, are not in reality homœopathic medicines at
all; they are simply elegant and ingenious little
vehicles for the administration of the various remedies
when reduced to the liquid form (tincture), and used
on the same principle as Doctor Dosewell selects
honey, syrup, jam, or jelly for his nauseous compound
of grey powder, rhubarb, senna, or Dover's powder
in quovis vehiculo crasso—in some convenient vehicle ;

or as once facetiously translated by a candidate for the licence of the Apothecaries' Company—in some stout Hackney coach.

On the Selection of Remedies.

The fundamental principle of homœopathic practice —the law of cure—as discovered, demonstrated, and promulgated by Hahnemann, is simply and forcibly expressed in the following maxim:—Similia similibus curantur, which simply means that diseases are cured most quickly, safely, and effectually, by medicines which are capable of producing symptoms SIMILAR to those existing in the patient, and which characterize his disease ; for in accordance with the therapeutic law of similarity, medicines cure affections similar or like unto those they produce. The immortal bard of Avon has well expressed this law in the following lines :—

> "Tut, man ! one fire burns out another's burning,
> One pain is lessened by another's anguish.
> Turn giddy, and be holp by backward turning ;
> One desperate grief cures with another's languish :
> Take thou some new infection to the eye,
> And the rank poison of the old will die."

Homœopathy, then, proceeds upon the great incontrovertible truth, that as the phenomena of chemistry depend upon positive laws—as the movements and instincts of the brute creation are regulated in the most orderly manner—as the physiological functions of the human organism constitute an harmonious play of beautifully co-ordinate forces,—so nature has ordained a definite relation between *remedial* agents and *diseases*. In the discoveries of such relationship,

extending over a field co-extensive with Nature herself, ever fresh, ever increasing in interest, consists the
study of homœopathy in its application as well as
its practice.   The treatment of disease henceforth
must rest on positive and unerring laws ; it cannot
possibly depend on chance, but must be regulated in a
manner commensurate with the unchanging principles
of nature and philosophy.

While the differences of sexes in all living beings
beneficently bind them together in prolific union, the
crude matters of inorganic nature are impelled by
like instincts.   Even in the darkness of chaos, matter
was accumulated or separated accordingly as affinity
or antagonistic matter attracted or repelled its various
parts.   The celestial fire follows the metals, the
magnet the iron ; amber when rubbed attracts light
bodies ; earth blends with earth ; salt separates from
the waters of the sea and joins its like.   Everything
in inanimate nature hastens to associate itself with its
like.

The beauteous aspect of the world, the order of
the celestial bodies, the revolution of the sun, the
moon, and all the stars, indicate sufficiently at one
glance that all this is not the work of chance.

Potencies.

Homœopathic medicines have been used by physicians at various dilutions,—from the mother tinctures
to the two thousandth attenuation ; for ordinary purposes, however, I would advise my readers to confine
their selections from the mother tincture ϕ to the
3rd x, or 6th x dilution, as being the most useful and

efficacious, and, moreover, in accordance with the views of the majority and more advanced sections of homœopathic practitioners in this country and America. They constitute the ordinary potencies prescribed by the writer for many years, and have proved eminently successful in his hands.

Mode of Administration.

We have observed that there are four modes of preparing the medicines — viz., Tinctures, Triturations, medicated Pilules and Globules; there is also more than one mode of administering these remedies.

TINCTURES.—The dose of these preparations is, as a rule, one drop administered at stated intervals.

In acute diseases, and in those severe and dangerous complaints which rapidly run their headlong course to a fatal termination, as, for instance, croup, cholera, acute atrophy of the liver, &c., it may be necessary at the commencement of the treatment to repeat the dose at intervals of every ten, twenty, or thirty minutes, until a favourable impression is made on the symptoms, when the interval between the doses should be lengthened as the patient improves. For this purpose it were well to mix thoroughly twelve drops of the selected tincture in twelve tablespoonfuls of water, and administer accordingly.

In chronic diseases there should be an interval between the repetition of the dose of from twelve to twenty-four hours; and according to the strict rules of Hahnemann, to as many days or weeks. This prolonged action of one dose of a medicine has been much doubted: I have but little faith in it myself,

and generally advise that the medicine should be
repeated once a day, or night and morning.

TRITURATIONS.—These preparations may be taken
dry on the tongue, or in solution : one grain, or as
much as will stand on the point of a penknife, is,
about equal to one drop of the tincture, one pilule,
or six globules.

If the solution be preferred, twelve grains should
be dissolved in twelve table-spoonfuls of water, well
stirred, and taken according to the circumstances of
the case.

PILULES AND GLOBULES.—These elegant and
liliputian medicaments may also be taken either dry
on the tongue or in solution. If the former, one
pilule or six globules may be considered a fair adult
dose ; if the latter, one pilule or six globules dissolved in a table-spoonful of water may be considered
equivalent to one drop of the tincture in the same
quantity of water.

Medicines, as a rule, should be taken on an empty
stomach, or about two hours after a meal.

The water used for mixing the medicine should be
distilled, filtered, or cold boiled.

The solution should be made in a clean tumbler,
closely covered with half a sheet of note-paper, or in a
bottle well corked and kept from dust and light.

Diet.

All articles of diet and drinks which contain
medicinal properties should be strictly avoided whilst
taking homœopathic medicines, such as coffee, green
tea, and herb teas of every description ; ginger,

pepper, vinegar, mustard, allspice, cinnamon, cloves and spices of all kinds; every variety of vegetable food of an aromatic or medicinal character, as onions, garlic, radishes, celery, or parsnips ; and every variety of animal food strong-scented or difficult of digestion, as old smoked meat, roof beef, bacon, fat pork, sausages, rancid butter, strong cheese, &c.

In acute diseases the diet should consist of the most light and nutritious sorts of food, such as toast-water, barley-water, rice-water, panada, arrowroot, gruel, and mutton broth. When the more violent symptoms of the disease have subsided, and the patient is fairly convalescent, more substantial food may be allowed in moderate quantities, such as beef tea or chicken tea, thickened with pearl barley, arrowroot, or sago, boiled rice, boiled chicken, or a sweetbread, toast, rice and bread pudding, and if there exists no derangement of the stomach or bowels, a few grapes, strawberries, or peaches may be taken. In chronic diseases, almost every variety of wholesome, nutritious, and easily digested food may be allowed, providing it does not answer the description of such kinds of aliments as are above prohibited.

As an ordinary beverage pure water should be allowed in all cases, toast-water, apple-water, barley-water, or rice-water, with an occasional glass of sound Burgundy, Carlowitz, or Somlau.

LIST OF MEDICINES

PRESCRIBED IN THIS WORK; THEIR NUMBER, OFFICIAL NAMES, ABBREVIATIONS, AND
THE POTENCY USUALLY PRESCRIBED BY THE AUTHOR.

No.	Official Name	Abbreviation	English Name	Potency
1	Aconitum Napellus	Acon.	Monkshood	
2	Acidum Nitricum	Ac. N.	Nitric Acid	
3	Antimonium Tartaricum	Ant. T.	Tartar Emetic	
4	Arsenicum Album	Ars. A.	White Arsenic	
5	Aurum Metallicum	Aur. M.	Pure Gold	
6	Belladonna	Bell.	Deadly Nightshade	
7	Cannabis Sativa	Cann. M.	Hemp	
8	Camphora	Camph.	Camphor	
9	Cantharis Vesicatoria	Canth.	Spanish Fly	
10	Causticum	Caust.		
11	Clematis Erecta	Clem.	Upright Virgin's Bower	
12	Chamomilla	Mor.	Hydrargyri Nitrico-Oxydum	

No.	Name	Abbrev.	English			
13	China Officinalis ...	Chin. ...	Cinchona, or Peruvian Bark ...	0 1	2	3
14	Dulcamara (Solanum) ...	Dulc. ...	Woody Nightshade ...	0 1		3
15	Ferri Potassio Tartras ...	Fer. P. T.	Tartrate of Potash and Iron ...	0 1	2	3
16	Ferrum Iodidum ...		Iodide of Iron ...	0 1	2	
17	Hamamelis Virginica ...	Hama. ...	Witch Hazel ...	0 1	2	3
18	Hepar Sulphuris ...	Hep. S. ...	Liver of Sulphur ...	0 1	2	3
19	Iodide Potassi, vel Kali Hydriodicum ...		Iodide of Potassium ...	0 1	2	
20	Kreasotum ...		Creasote ...	0 2	3	
21	Lycopodium Claratum ...	Lycop. ...	Common Club Moss ...	0 2	3	
22	Mercurius biniodidus ...	Merc. b. Iod. ...	Biniodide of Mercury ...	0 1	2	3
23	Mercurius Sulphuratus Ruber...	Cinnab. ...	Vermilion ...	0 1	2	3
24	Mercurius Nitratis ...	Merc. N. ...	Nitrate of Mercury ...	0 1	2	3
25	Mercurius Phosphatus ...		Phosphate of Mercury ...	0 1	2	3
26	Mercurius Solubilis ...		Hahnemann's Soluble Mercury ...	0 1	2	3
27	Mercurius Vivus ...		Quicksilver ...	0 1	3	
28	Nux Vomica ...	Nux V.	Nux Vomica ...	0 1	6	
29	Platina ...	Plat. ...	Platinum ...	0 1	2	3
30	Pulsatilla Nigricans...	Puls. ...	Wind-flower ...	0 1	2	3
31	Petroselinum Sativum ...	Petros. ...	Parsley ...	0 1	2	
32	Rhus Toxicodendron ...	Rhus ...	Poison Oak ...	0 1	2	
33	Sar Saparilla ...	Sar Z. ...	Sarsaparilla ...	0 1	2	3
34	Sabina ...	Sabin. ...	Savine ...	0 1	2	3
35	Staphysagria ...	Staph. ...	Stavesacre ...	0 1	6	12
36	Silicea ...	Sil. ...	Pure Flint ...	0 1	3	6
37	Sulphur ...	Sulph. ...	Sulphur ...	0 1	2	3
38	Thuja Occidentalis ...	Thuja ...	Tree of Life ...			

LIST OF MEDICINES

PRESCRIBED IN THIS WORK; THEIR NUMBER, OFFICIAL NAMES, ABBREVIATIONS, AND THE POTENCY USUALLY PRESCRIBED BY THE AUTHOR.

No.	Official Name	Abbreviation	English Name	Potency
1	Aconitum Napellus	Acon.	Monkshood	φ 1 2 3
2	Acidum Nitricum	Ac. N.	Nitric Acid	φ 1 2 3
3	Antimonium Tartaricum	Ant. T.	Tartar Emetic	φ 1 2 3
4	Arsenicum Album	Ars. A.	White Arsenic	2 3 6
5	Aurum Metallicum	Aur. M.	Pure Gold	3 6
6	Belladonna	Bell.	Deadly Nightshade	φ 1 2 3
7	Cannabis Sativa	Can. S.	Hemp	φ 1 2 3
8	Camphora	Camph.	Camphor	φ φ
9	Cantharis Vesicatoria	Canth.	Spanish Fly	1 2 3
10	Causticum	Caust.		3 6
11	Clematis Erecta	Clem.	Upright Virgin's Bower	φ 1 2 3
12	Cinnabaris	See.	Hydrargyri Nitrico-Oxydum	3 6

No.	Name	Abbrev.	English Name	φ	1	2	3
13	China Officinalis	Chin....	Cinchona, or Peruvian Bark	φ	1	2	3
14	Dulcamara (Solanum)	Dulc....	Woody Nightshade		1	2	3
15	Ferri Potassio Tartras	Fer. P. T.	Tartrate of Potash and Iron	φ			
16	Ferrum Iodidum		Iodide of Iron		1	2	3
17	Hamamelis Virginica	Hama.	Witch Hazel	φ	1	2	3
18	Hepar Sulphuris	Hep. S.	Liver of Sulphur		1	2	3
19	Iodide Potassi, vel Kali Hy-driodicum		Iodide of Potassium	φ	1	2	
20	Kreasotum		Creasote		2	3	
21	Lycopodium Claratum	Lycop.	Common Club Moss		2	3	
22	Mercurius biniodidus	Merc. b. Iod.	Biniodide of Mercury		2	3	
23	Mercurius Sulphuratus Ruber..	Cinnab.	Vermilion		1	2	3
24	Mercurius Nitratis	Merc. N.	Nitrate of Mercury		2	3	
25	Mercurius Phosphatus		Phosphate of Mercury		2	3	
26	Mercurius Solubilis		Hahnemann's Soluble Mercury	φ	1	2	
27	Mercurius Vivus		Quicksilver	φ		3	
28	Nux Vomica	Nux V.	Nux Vomica		2	3	
29	Platina	Plat.	Platinum	φ		3	
30	Pulsatilla Nigricans..	Puls.	Wind-flower	φ	1	2	3
31	Petroselinum Sativum	Petros.	Parsley	φ	1	2	3
32	Rhus Toxicodendron	Rhus...	Poison Oak	φ	1	2	
33	Sar Saparilla	Sar Z.	Sarsaparilla		2	3	
34	Sabina	Sabin.	Savine		2	3	
35	Staphysagria	Staph.	Stavesacre	φ	1	2	3
36	Silicea	Sil.	Pure Flint	φ	1	6	12
37	Sulphur	Sulph.	Sulphur		3	6	
38	Thuja Occidentalis	Thuja	Tree of Life	φ	1	2	3

HISTORY OF SYPHILIS.

ALTHOUGH it is by no means difficult to follow out
the modern progress and dissemination of syphilis
and its allied disorders, the early history of the
complaint is nevertheless a somewhat intricate task,
and has required the united researches of a numerous
body of able men at various eras, and in all civilised
countries ; but this evidence is at the present time in a
fair state of completeness, and may therefore be submitted with little fear that much may be altered in its
main features. This evidence we shall now set down
under the following heads : —

    1. Theory of *Endemic* origin.

    2. Theory of *American,* or St. Domingo origin.

    3. Theory of *African* introduction.

Let us therefore briefly consider these in the order
so arranged. According to the theory of *Endemic*
origin, syphilis, in a more or less virulent form, has
existed from the very earliest times of which mankind
has any kind of knowledge, either traditional or
historical.

CHINA.—According to the testimony of Forneau,
a learned French Jesuit, the Chinese authorities refer

to its existence among their nation from time
immemorial; and the remarkable work of Captain
Dabray, (*La Médecine Chez-les Chinois*), published
1863, contains a mass of evidence extracted from their
medical writings, some of which ascend to the
Hoang-ty dynasty, 2-637 years B.C., that syphilis was
well known in that ancient country. *Chancres, and
corroding ulcers* of the genital organs, the *mouth, throat,
nose,* and *rectum,* are freely spoken of as arising from a
specific poison communicated by direct contact, and
appearing from the third to the ninth day. *Secondary*
and *tertiary* lesions are also pretty freely described, as
sanious discharge, ulceration, and destruction of the
Septum Nasi, nodes on the bones, &c.

INDIA.—The *Sucrutas Ayuvedas,* an historic
work on Hindoo medicine written A.D. 400, contains
many passages referring to *Syphilis. Chancre* is mentioned with its loathsome train of horrors, as *ozœna,
warts, nodes* and *buboes,* for which a system of treatment
is clearly laid down. F. C. Klein, in a series of papers
published in the *Journ. de Médec.* 1795, contends,
from the history of Malabar, that it is more than nine
centuries since syphilis was first named, and *Mercury*
given as a cure. But the complaint, if we may trust
to Strabo, Diodorus, and Pliny, was comparatively rare
in India in their time, doubtless from their plain mode
of living and cleanliness. It may be as well to state
that the Indian codes of law regulating marriages and
sexual intercourse do not appear to have been
influenced by any fear on this head; the principle of
castes was purely religious, and dictated by notions of
policy of a widely different nature.

BIBLICAL REFERENCES.—Several authors both ancient and modern, have endeavoured to link *syphilitic*
and *syphiloidal* diseases with certain passages in Holy
Writ, such as the running issue out of the flesh;
the sores covering the body from the sole of the foot
to the crown of the head ; the *Baal-peor* plague transmitted to the Israelites by the daughters of the
Midianites, and which was of so malignant a character
that *twenty-four thousand* of them died in a very short
time, for the isolation and careful treatment of which
Moses, in the fifteenth chapter of Leviticus, lays down
such stringent rules.

PERSIA.—The great historian Herodotus, whose
travels extended over a vast area, and whose general
veracity all modern researches are continually tending
to prove more and more unimpeachably, refers to
certain diseases among the Persians (i. cap. 139). He
speaks of those under the terms λεπρα and λεύκη
respectively *Lepra* and *Leuke*, the latter signifying
white ; hence is derived the modern term *Leucorrhœa*
for woman's whites. If, however, we bear in mind that
the Persians, the Babylonians, the Massageta, and the
Scythians practised indiscriminate sexual intercourse,
and that in the grossest and most unblushing manner, it
is far more probable that the *Leuke* applied to sexual
disorders was of a more or less virulent character ; and
hence, on the authority of a writer who was alive in the
fourth century B.C., we have clear traditional accounts in
a written form of the existence of something distinct
from *Lepra* in times long anterior to his own. The
salacity of the Eastern nations, in ancient as well as
modern times, arising from climate, is a matter of

world-wide fame ; and what we know of ancient times, as handed down by historians, whose veracity is beyond doubt, confirms us in the inference that the torrid and arid regions of the globe have always been cursed with these diseases, in a more or less virulent form. To this may we fairly attribute the rigid personal cleanliness, the bathing, and the shaving strictly enjoined as a religious duty by the priest-physicians of Egypt and adjacent countries.

GREECE.—Hippocrates, the renowned physician of ancient Cos, who flourished some 450 years before the Christian era, in his work on Epidemics (book iii., section 3, cap. 7), refers to *ulcers* and *warts* (thymia) which break out on the sexual organs, and recommends for the removal of the latter the *Pyrethrum parthenium*, or fever-few, and *Alum.*

ROME.—Celsus, one of the oldest Latin medical writers, devotes a whole chapter to the consideration of the various forms of venereal affections ; and refers to dry and moist ulcers, the former clean, the latter purulent, the *chancre* and *chancroid* of the present day. He also refers to *serpiginous* and *phagedænic* sores ; ulcers on the *nose, mouth,* and *tonsils.* Aretæus of Cappadocia backs up Celsus as to secondary symptoms, and refers to the uvula being destroyed to the bones of the palate, and the fauces to the root of the tongue and epiglottis. Galen and Ætius respectively mention psoriasis of the scrotum, pustules and ulcers on the pudendum. Plutarch and Marcellus Empiricus refer to *tertiary* symptoms in the form of ulcerated and serpiginous affections of the tibia, and deep-seated bone pains.

JUDEA.—The Jewish historian Josephus speaks
of the private parts of Herod that had become putrid,
and likewise of a corrosive ulcer on the private parts
of the blasphemer Apion, which cost him his life; this
may have been the *phagedænic* or *gangrenous* sore of
the present day.

I. SYPHILIS IN THE MIDDLE AGES.

Passing from ancient times to the Middle Ages, we
find, ample proof that *syphilis* is not to be regarded as
a recent disease, as formerly alleged. A manuscript
of the *ninth century* discovered by Darenburg contains
a reference showing an evident connection between
diseases of the anus and those of the genital organs.
Ulcers on the genitals were well described about the
same time by the Arabian physicians Rhazes,
Avicenna, and Albucasis, and many others all over
Europe. Both *soft* and *hard* sores on the prepuce are
mentioned by Lanfranc, of Milan, in his *Chirurgie*,
A.D. 1270, and chancres in both sexes are well
described by Valescus at a somewhat later period.
A cloud of contemporary, or immediately succeeding
writers might be cited in reference to this point, did
space permit our doing so. It may, however, be
sufficient here to refer to the labours of Arnauld de
Villeneuve, Theodoric, Trotula, together with the
poets Villon, and Pacificus Maximus. Secondary
symptoms are distinctly referred to in manuscripts of
the thirteenth century, especially by Gerard du Berri,
in his *Glossulæ*, where the whole system is stated to
be thus infected, but generally associated with forms
of lepra; whilst John of Gadisden an English

physician of considerable repute in his time, clearly showed that diseases of the genital organs had arisen from *lepra*. In fact, leprosy and syphilis in those early days seem to have arisen from like causes.

Pierre Martyn, in April, 1488, writes on the subject to his friend Arias Barbosa as follows, which seems clear and conclusive :—" You tell me," says he, " that you are afflicted with a particular disease, called *Bubas* by the Spaniards ; *Gallico* by the Italians ; *Elephantiasis* by some physicians, and in various ways by others. You describe, with incomparable elegance, your evils, your losses, the uneasiness in your joints, the weakness of your ligaments, the excruciating pains in your articulations, and lastly, the ulcers and fœtor of your breath." The sympto-matology of syphilis is here depicted in the strongest language, and an hypothesis we have advanced in this work receives strong support from its ultimating in cirrhosis, softening of the brain, and idiotcy. But the enormous impulse this disease received at the end of the *fifteenth century* should not be omitted as clearly pointing out its epidemic and contagious properties. In 1493-4 it showed itself in the following distant localities : Auvergne, Lombardy, Brandenburg, Bruns-wick, Mecklenburg, Prussia, Westphalia, Pomerania, Suabia, Franconia, Bavaria, Paris, Rome, Dalmatia, Macedonia, and Greece ; one-twentieth of the popu-lation on an average being afflicted with it.

Jerome Fracastorius, a native of Verona, in a work entitled *De Morbis Contagiosis*, published at Venice in 1546, gives a most vivid picture of the early symptoms of this great epidemic, which are worth

recording. "Amongst other wonderful phenomena,"
says that author, "which have happened in this age,
we have seen a disease spring up quite new and long
unknown in this part of the world, which has over-
spread almost all Europe, and likewise a great part of
Asia and Africa ; but in Italy it broke out about the
year 1490, at the time when the French took possession
of the kingdom of Naples under their king, Charles.
In some persons the disease commenced without
contagion ; in others, and these were the greater
number, it was transmitted by contagion. Not
every kind of contact sufficed for producing it; it
required that two bodies should become heated
together, as occurs in the act of coition. And it
was chiefly by coition that the greater number became
infected. However, a considerable number of children
contracted the disease by suckling diseased mothers
or nurses. The disease was not communicable at
a distance, it did not show itself immediately, but
sometimes at the end of one, two, or even four months ;
certain signs, however, announced already that
the disease was in the germ.

"Those affected were sad, weary, and cast down;
they were pale, most of them had sores on the genital
organs, ulcers similar to those which are wont to
develop themselves on those organs after coition, and
which are called *caries*, but of a very different nature ;
they were obstinate. When they were cured in one
place they appeared in another, and the treatment
had to be recommenced. Afterwards pustules arose
on the skin, covered with a crust : in some they
appeared upon the head, which was the most frequent

place ; in others they appeared elsewhere. At first they were small, afterwards they increased to the size of an acorn, which they resembled in shape, their appearance otherwise being similar to the *crusta lactea* of children. In some cases these pustules were small and dry ; in others, they were large and moist ; in some livid ; in others, whitish and rather pale ; in others, hard and reddish. They always broke in a few days, and constantly discharged an incredible quantity of stinking matter as soon as open ; they were so many true *phagedænic* ulcers which destroyed not only the flesh, but even the bones. Those attacked in the upper parts of the body suffered from malignant affections, which ate away sometimes the *palate*, sometimes the *fauces*, sometimes the *larynx*, sometimes the *tonsils ;* some lost the *lips*, others the *nose*, others all the *genital* organs. Many had *gummy* tumours on the limbs, which disfigured them, and were often of the size of an egg, or of a small loaf. When they broke, a kind of white mucilaginous fluid flowed from them. They chiefly attacked the arms and legs ; sometimes they remained callous till death. But as. if all this were not sufficient, there ensued, moreover, severe pains in the limbs, often at the same time with pustules ; sometimes before, sometimes after them. These pains, which were persistent and unbearable, were chiefly felt in the night, and were seated in the limbs themselves, and in the nerves rather than in the joints. Some, however, had pustules without the pains, others pains without the pustules, and most had both pustules and pains. However, all the limbs were in a languid condition. The patients were wan and emaciated, without appetite, sleepless, always melancholy and ill-humoured, and anxious to remain in bed. Their faces and legs swelled, and a slow fever sometimes supervened, but rarely. Some suffered pains in the head, which were persistent, and did not yield to any remedy. If blood was drawn it was found to be pure, and somewhat mucous; the urine was thick and red: by this sign alone, supervening in the absence of fever, the disease might be recognised. The stools were liquid and mucous."

Such were the symptoms of the disease at its commencement. But I speak of a past time; for now, although the disease is still prevalent, it nevertheless appears to differ from what it was then. We have seen during about the last twenty years *fewer pustules* and more *gummy tumours*, which is the reverse of what was observed in the first years. The *pustules*, when any appear, are drier, and the pains, when any supervene, more severe. Within about six years the disease has again changed notably. We now see *pustules* in but very few patients; scarcely any pains, or much lighter ones, but many *gummy tumours*.

A circumstance which has astonished everybody is the falling off of the hair of the head and other parts of the body, which produces a ridiculous appearance; some have no *beard*, some no *eyebrows*, and some are *bald*. At first these results were attributed to the remedies, especially to *mercury*.

Now it is still worse; in many the teeth become loose, and in many they even fall out.

This pestilential character it did not, however, maintain for more than seven years; the great wave of the

disease had spent itself and passed away within that
brief period, assuming by degrees a less virulent form,
while the epidemic form of the malady had disappeared, according to the evidence of a large number
of authorities, towards the middle or the end of the sixteenth century.   Ricord is disposed to connect this
epidemic with certain forms of *glanders*, *farcy*, and
such like disorders.   In our own day the malignancy
of *syphilis* has undoubtedly revived, and it would be
instructive to compare modern cases with the statements made by those eminent authorities who observed
it in its then great intensity, a comparison of which
our limits do not at present admit.

In bringing this portion of the history of syphilis to
a close, and without absolutely subscribing to the
endemic character of that dire complaint, nevertheless
we are certainly entitled to regard these authorities as
possessing no slight degree of weight.   Assuming it
to be of endemic origin, this evidence to be of similar
importance to that derived from other sources, it would
appear by no means improbable that the disease was
absolutely rooted in nature itself; and those who
unhesitatingly accept the *genetical* account of the
origin of the evil may see in it the points of man's
first disobedience.   Probably, if the modern doctrine
of the *polygenetic* origin of mankind be accepted, we
might find it rising up at equal periods of civilization
among all the races of man in the different centres of
original emergence.

2. THEORY OF AMERICAN OR ST. DOMINGO ORIGIN.

This theory as to the origin of syphilis has been

strenuously maintained by many learned men, and as indignantly repelled by as many more. They ascribe its first appearances in Europe to the sailors of Columbus on their return home from the island of Hispaniola, now known as San Domingo.

But it is hardly fair to impute the origin of such a disease to the harmless and primitive race inhabiting that island at the time, comparatively a mere speck in the great Atlantic Ocean; nor does it seem likely that so terrible a scourge, which habits of uncleanliness materially aggravate, should have arisen among a race conspicuous for bathing and swimming, and other methods of ridding the body of foul humours. And again, it would seem monstrous that to one small area should be confined a VIRUS so foul in its nature, and destructive in its properties, as to have killed and maimed more victims than have fallen by the sword and cannon from the days of Crecy to the ever-memorable siege of Paris in 1870-1.

It is much more compatible with common sense and experience to find a disease of such a nature taking its rise among an effete and heterogeneous population such as we find Europe to possess at the era of its sudden dissemination, that is, if we propose to accept the theory of its novelty at all. For more than thirty years after its appearance no author ever dreamt of attributing the origin of syphilis to a West Indian isle.

3. THEORY OF AFRICAN INTRODUCTION.

A still more startling theory was propounded by Leonardo Fioravanti of Bologna in a treatise entitled

Capricci Medicinali, 1564, who affirms that he was informed by the son of a sutler who was in the army of Alphonso V., King of Arragon, while contending for the kingdom of Naples in 1456, that being distressed for provisions, the two opposing armies were supplied with dressed human flesh, and hence arose the malady; and Francis Bacon, Lord Verulam, added to this that the flesh was that of men killed in Barbary, prepared in a similar way to tunny fish. That this theory is, however, untenable is demonstrated by facts derivable from the history of cannibalism in general; and it is consequently safer to conclude with Clavigero, that "as nobody knew, nor could know, who was the first in Europe that suffered that great evil, neither can we know the original cause of it." Without absolutely binding ourselves to the hypothesis of its introduction from Africa, it must be confessed that the filthy and degraded habits of the negro render the theory of its having arisen in the equatorial regions of Africa at least tenable. It is universally admitted that the lucrative trade carried on for centuries with those regions incited many Europeans to resort to African markets for the purpose of traffic and barter; and the unbridled licence of the time may have caused the rude sailors of the European fleets to contract something of an infectious nature, from the unnatural intermixture of two such opposite races. It should also be borne in mind that the appearance of that terrible scourge in Europe falls within the period of the greatest commercial activity of the Venetians and Genoese, whose trade with Egypt, and so with Africa, was then at its height.

Before drawing my remarks on the history of syphilis to a close, I would by way of curiosity briefly refer to other causes assigned to it by some learned though superstitious writers of that period.

In 1497 Coradinus Gilinus, in 1500 Gaspar Torella, and in 1502 Wendelinus Brakenaw took an astronomical view of the matter, and ascribed it to the near conjunction of the sun with Jupiter, Saturn, and Mercury, an event which took place about these periods.

In 1497 Nicholas Leonicenus attributed its appearance to the abundant rains and inundations which occurred in Italy in the year the contagion first appeared.

In 1525 John Maynard ascribed it to the impure conversation of a leprous gentleman of Valencia with a courtezan; and Paracelsus assigned it a similar cause.

In 1551 Bravasolus of Ferrara, with more likelihood, attributed it to a courtezan in Naples during the French occupation, who had at the time an abscess in the mouth of the uterus.

In 1560 Gabriel Fallopius affirmed that the Spanish soldiers during that war poisoned the wells of the French, and bribed the Italian bakers who were in the invaders' army to mix lime with their bread, and hence originated the scourge.

Another theory which has found many supporters attributes the origin of syphilis to the Mariani, as they were called, an immense multitude of Jews, some 400,000 in number, who were expelled from Spain in 1492, wandered into Italy and settled down before

the gates of Rome, by permission of Pope Alexander
VI., when upwards of 30,000 perished from a pestilential Typhus, accompanied by the exhibition of large
pustules, which broke out among them.   But considering that an Act of Parliament was passed in Paris in
1496 alluding to the great pox, *Grosse vérole* as
having already existed for more than two years, and
some time before Charles VIII. and his army reached
the walls of Naples, and considering also that the
disease was well known in Westphalia in 1492, the
Mariani theory with many others must fall to the
ground.

In conclusion, I cannot refrain from directing attention to the following brief extracts gleaned from a
series of important and ingenious papers by one
William Beckett, an English surgeon, on "The Antiquity of the Venereal Disease," which the reader will
find in the 30th and 31st vols. of the Philosophical
Transactions, A.D. 1718 and 1720.   They are models
of research, and contain references to every printed
or written document published in the British Isles,
with the assistance of which he endeavoured to prove
that every form of *Venereal disease* was well known in
England centuries before the outbreak of the great
epidemic at Naples in 1493 and 4 ; and what is most
remarkable in the literary labours of that man
is, the number of cases recorded as having been
caused by intercourse with LEPROUS women, on
which account strict injunctions were laid down
against all sexual intercourse with women thus
diseased.

In his first dissertation he proves the existence

of a *Venereal Gonorrhœa* as having been known in England ages before 1490, and refers—

1. To a manuscript treatise by John Arden, Surgeon to King Richard II. and Henry IV. (pub. 1370), who, speaks of the disease as *ardor, arsura,* and *incendium ;* anglicised *brenning,* or *burning.*

2. To certain other manuscripts, written about 1390, containing prescriptions and other formulas for the treatment of such *brenning* or *burning* both in men and women.

3. To the rules and ordinances of the stews, or licensed brothels, published as far back as 1162. These stews, eighteen in number, were situate on the bankside, Southwark, and were under the jurisdiction of the Bishop of Winchester in the reign of Henry VIII. as follows :—

"De his qui custodiant mulieres habentes Nefandam infirmitatem."

A. No stew holder to take more for a woman's chamber for the week than fourteen pence.

B. Not to keep open his doors upon holy-days.

C. No single woman to be kept against her will, that would leave her sin.

D. No single woman to take money to lie with any man, except she lie with him all night till the morning.

E. No stew holder to keep any woman that hath the *perilous infirmity* of *burning,* but that she be put out, upon the pain of making a fine unto the Lord * of one hundred shillings.

4. To a manuscript by one Simon Fish, a zealous promoter of the Reformation, entitled " The Supplica-

---

* The Bishop of the diocese.

tion of Beggars," presented to Henry VIII. 1530;
wherein he says, speaking of the priests :—

"These be they your Majesty, that corrupt the whole
generation of mankind in your Realm, that catch the
Pokes of one woman and bear them to another."

5. To a work by Andrew Boord, M.D., and Romish
priest, entitled "The Breviary of Health," pub. 1546,
wherein references are made to the same subject.

6. To a manuscript by John Ball, M.D., pub. 1556,
which Beckett had in his collection of Ancient British
Works.

7. To a treatise by M. Wood, M.D., pub. 1553.

8. To a book by W. Bulleim, M.D., Physician to
Queen Elizabeth, entitled the "Bulwark of Health,"
1562, wherein references are made to a *brenning* or
burning, signifying in the present day a *gonorrhœa* or
clap.

From these and many more instances Beckett maintained that a *venereal gonorrhœa* was recognized in the
British isles from times immemorial under the desig-
nation of *ardor*, *ursura*, and *incendium*.

In the second dissertation, published in 1720,
Beckett refers to another manuscript by John Arden,
curiously written on vellum, and beautifully illumi-
nated, wherein references are made to *Phymosis*, *Paraphymosis*, and a *Caruncle-quere chancre*, sometimes
found in the urethra; to a certain Rector who had
warts growing on the glans; to another who had a
substance as big as a small strawberry growing on the
same part of the organ, which proceeded from the
corrupted matter in the urethra; to contumacious
chancres on the glans, and the difficulty found in curing

them; to buboes in the groins called Dorsers; to nodes on the shin-bones, termed *Boonhaw*, the old English word *Hawe* signifying a swelling; to falling off of the hair; hoarseness of the voice; ulcers all over the body; corruption of the fleshy parts, and of the bones themselves; filthy ulcers of the throat, corrosion and falling in of the nose, all of which would yield to no other remedy but MERCURY.

9. To a remarkable manuscript in Lincoln College, Oxford, written by the Chancellor of the University, A.D. 1430, viz.:—

"I Thomas Gascoigne an unworthy doctor of Divinity, who wrote and collected these observations, have known several men who have died of a putrefaction of the genitals, and of the whole body; which putrefaction and corruption as they said, was owing to carnal copulation. For that great English Duke, viz.: John of Gaunt, first named Plantagenet, died of a putrefaction of the kind, occasioned by coition. For he was much addicted to *venery*, as was well known all over England, and when he was upon his death bed he shewed that mortification to King Richard II.

"This was communicated to me by an honest Batchelor of Divinity who was the only person in the secret. Willis likewise a citizen of London, and pretty far advanced in years, died of a mortification of the same kind, occasioned by carnal copulation with lewd women, which he confessed to several persons before his death, as he was distributing alms with his own hands, of which I was a witness in the year 1430."

From these and similar observations, William Beckett maintained that TRUE SYPHILIS also existed in

the British Isles, as well as elsewhere, centuries anterior
to its supposed introduction into Europe by the sailors
of Columbus.

ANALOGOUS DISEASES TO SYPHILIS.

AFRICA.—Large portions of that benighted country
have for ages past been cursed with severe forms of
venereal diseases, known as *Yaws, Pian,* and *Frambesia.*
It was referred to by the Arabian physicians
as early as the tenth century, under the name of
Sahafati. It seems to have committed great ravages
along the left bank of the Senegal, Congo, Senegambia,
and Sierra Leone. It confines itself chiefly to individuals
of the Negrotian type —rarely amongst the white.

SCOTLAND also has been the theatre of an
analogous disorder, known as SIBBENS or SEWENS. It
first appeared A.D. 1694, breaking out almost simultaneously
in the counties of Galloway, Dumfries,
Wigton, and Ayr. It is now almost extinct. It presented
the usual signs of syphilis—namely, ulcers on
the genitals, *buboes, nodes, bone pains,* and *spongy
fungous excrescences,* all of which yielded to MERCURY.

SWEDEN and NORWAY have long been cursed
with a very disgusting form of the venereal, named
Radesyge, which, according to that eminent syphilographer,
Boack of Christiania, is identical to true
syphilis. Its chief indications are *throat ulcers, fleshy
excrescences* about anus and genitals, indurated glands,
bone pains, caries of the nasal bones, and exostosis. It
is highly contagious, and yields chiefly to MERCURY.

: JUTLAND, HOLSTEIN, ETHONIA, COURLAND, and

LITHUANIA were visited, some century and a half ago, by a disease of a *syphiloidal* nature, which was chiefly transmitted by means of spoons, drinking-vessels, clothes, and bedding. It presented itself chiefly in the form of mucous tubercles.

AMBOYNA is likewise the seat of a severe form of syphilis, known as *Amboyna pimple.* It is endemic throughout the Molucca and Java Islands. It presents itself in the form of *ulcers* with *hard raised edges,* pains and caries in the bones, and may be communicated to others independently of sexual intercourse.

CANADA.—In 1760 a syphiloidal complaint appeared in Canada, and committed frightful ravages among the Ottawa Indians on Lake Huron, and like the syphiloidal of the Moluccas, was easily transmitted by pipes, bed-linen, and drinking-vessels. It presented all the symptoms of syphilis, caries of the bones being a marked feature.

Can Syphilis Arise Without Contagion?

It has been long a *vexata questio* as to the possibility of syphilis arising without absolute contagion.

Taking the French and German writers as the best authorities, this disease unquestionably assumes the specific character of *cachexia*, and the acrimony and density of the virus is a marked feature.

Astruc * very properly alludes to the *venereal poison* as being of a *morbific acid* and *corrosive nature*. That personal carelessness produces not alone the terrible symptoms so well known as scarcely to require definition cannot be doubted, and it is even probable that the fearful complaint, which has hitherto baffled the skill of the whole faculty of the world, known as cancer, has arisen from some such similar causes. In CELIBATE persons of both sexes, for instance, it has been frequently observed, ultimately to the neglect of personal cleanliness. The almost veneration paid by many to the organs affected has led to such neglect. *Melancholia* has occasionally exhibited itself, and the symptomatology points to its perhaps proximate rise in the misdirected and inverted ideas as to chastity.

"It is better," says St. Paul, "to marry than burn," and prurient religious excitement has been known so to excite the mind as to induce awful disarrangements of the framework of nature.

* Book ii., cap. 2.

It will undoubtedly display itself, either as INSANITY from disappointed affections, and the suppression of natural and healthy excretions ; or as CANCER ; or, as otherwise, LEPRA. Inflammation sets in, and the unfortunate sufferers labour under *bone pains, ulcers,* and other horrors. *Dyscrasia* sets in, and the degeneration leads further into the ultimate production of the most virulent forms of the disease. Clavigero, of whom we have here made considerable use,* is expressly of opinion that the evil may be produced without "any contagion or communication with those infected, because it can absolutely be generated in the same manner as it was generated in the first person who suffered from it ; such person could not get it by *contagion*, because he would not in that case have been the first who suffered it, but from another cause very different ; therefore, by a similar cause, whatever it was, some *cachexia* might have been produced without contagion in other individuals of the human species."

Insufficient or a degraded diet are among the causes assigned by Astruc. We have in Shakespeare's "King Lear" a cause assigned by Edgar for his feigned insanity, in his diet of—

"Rats and mice, and such small deer,"

and we are entitled to give respectful consideration to the inductions of a man whose usual insight has led to many important discoveries. It can scarcely be doubted that there is a direct and rational connection between sexual and cerebral disturbances, and that

* See Dissertation ix., section 3.

the repression of instincts, natural and healthy in themselves, must ultimately lead to serious mischief.

The testimony of Blumenbach as to natural nocturnal emissions of a non-acrid character deserves a passing consideration. He, in his Anthropological Treatises,* says that he regards nocturnal pollutions as natural excretions of the healthy man, to the intent that he may be thereby freed from the annoyance and stimulus of superfluous semen when it is suitable to him on account of his temperament or constitution, being, therefore, an analogue of the menstrual discharge in the female, and consequently upon the prerogative exercised by man of copulation at will.

Recurring to the lower animals for an instant, we find, to take for instance, the rut of the stag associated with all the phenomena of MANIA—that desire to associate with the female which produces GORING—of blind, not unreasoning rage decidedly of similar origin to the ideas connected with NYMPHOMANIA and SATYRIASIS. From such *acridity* the symptoms of *lues venerea* might not uncommonly arise, and cases in which symptoms of *syphilis* have even shown themselves in the Quadrumana have been alleged.

This I have observed myself in the horse, the ass, and on several occasions in the dog, both male and female. "Extreme acrid seminal fluid," says Clavigero in another place, "*uteri estuantes* and virulent courses have never been wanting either." The human sperm is itself of the utmost *acridity*, and *might* be so exaggerated as to give rise to the *cachectic* symptoms referred to. Plethora, as well as suppression, might

* T. Bendyshe, M.A , *Anthropological Journal.*

also have been a cause, and history certainly points to a very different idea from that of an American origin, as before stated.

That, however, syphilis may have assumed its present formidable character in the last years of the fifteenth century is not to be disputed or denied. Other diseases have appeared in the world, run their course, and have died out again; such as the *black death*, the *plague*, the *sweating sickness*, and other similar *scourges*. Another class of diseases, at one time as much dreaded and almost as fatal as those just referred to, but which, by the genius of man and a wise Legislature, have " become so modified in form, lessened in virulence, and tractable to treatment, as to create at the present time but little anxiety, such as the *Asiatic cholera, typhus, typhoid, scarlatina, diphtheria*, and many more. By analogy, therefore, it may be possible so to modify that destructive element of *syphilis* that in the course of time the present age may prepare the way for its entire destruction in our posterity, though it may be deemed as somewhat Quixotic to anticipate so grand a revolution as the total annihilation and stamping out, as it were, of so *foul* and *destructive* a poison in our own times.

SUMMARY.

A brief review of the foregoing historical sketch will enable us to arrive at the following propositions and general conclusions :—

GEOGRAPHICALLY.—Syphilis has been found distributed in a more or less virulent form over almost the entire surface of the globe. On the coast of the Adriatic, the Baltic, the Molucca Islands, and Mexico, it attains such virulence and intensity as to bear a strong resemblance to the great epidemic of the fifteenth century.

ANTIQUITY.—Although a clear nosographical system of syphilis cannot be traced further back than the fifteenth century, nevertheless that disease in its varied forms appears to have been observed and clearly described at a much earlier period.

HYGIENICALLY.—Syphilis rages with greater frequency and greater virulence in proportion as prostitution is less watched over and cleanliness neglected. This has been fully verified in this country since the introduction of the Contagious Diseases Acts, as proved by copious statistics and the Parliamentary Blue-books.*

EPIDEMICALLY.—In addition to its ordinary form, syphilis sometimes presents itself under an epidemic or endemic form. The first of these forms is rare, and only appears under special circumstances ; the second is more general, and may be stigmatised as the usual form of syphilis and syphiloidal disease cropping up in certain localities in our large seaports and other towns, and where there is an agglomeration of individuals not yet acclimatised.

---

* See my Comments on the Contagious Diseases Acts (p. 169.).

PART I.

THE ANATOMICAL, PHYSIOLOGICAL, · PATHOLOGICAL, AND THERAPEUTIC CHARACTERISTICS OF VENEREAL DISEASES.

LET us now proceed to consider the divers forms of venereal diseases. By VENEREAL I wish it to be understood as embracing all those disorders conferred by Venus on her worshippers after an impure *coïtus*. These I shall embrace in three main subdivisions, namely,—

Gonorrhœa and its complications.

Chancroid and its complications.

Chancre, or " true syphilis," and its complications.

To these I would add a fourth, namely, the sycosis of Hahnemann, otherwise "warty excrescences." The two former, according to the views of the most eminent syphilographers of the present day, restrict their morbid properties to surface and locality ; the third, however, penetrates into the inmost recesses of the vital organs, and even enters into the very centre of the citadel of the soul itself; whilst the sycosis is looked upon as an affection occasioned or engendered by the presence of a gonorrhœa, a primary or secondary syphilitic lesion—in fact, a kind of papillary hypertrophy or vegetation.

GONORRHŒA.

This form of the "venereal" is essentially a local disease, but of an inflammatory and very painful kind. It has an especial affinity for mucous membranès, beyond which it seldom travels. It has, however, a remarkable faculty of transporting itself at will, and attacking various local and remote organs of the body endowed more or less with mucous membrane :— locally, the *epididymis, testicles, anus, prostate* and *inguinal* glands ; remotely the *pharynx, larynx, eyes,* and *nose ;* finally the *capsules* and *synovial* membranes as " gonorrhœal rheumatism."

The leading typical forms of gonorrhœa are :—

Firstly, synonymously—gonorrhœa spuria, external gonorrhœa, external blennorrhagia, or balanitis.

This is a form of gonorrhœa which attacks the under surface of the prepuce and corona glandis.

SYMPTOMS.—The patient first complains of uneasiness, with a sense of titillation and tenderness at the tip of the penis, accompanied by itching and tingling underneath the prepuce, followed by a swollen, inflammatory, and excoriated condition of the parts, first bedewed with a sero-mucous exudation, terminating in a thick muco-purulent pus, which at times strongly resembles that of gonorrhœa. The excoriated surfaces, now denuded of epithelium, occur in patches and fissures ; and are the seat of a burning, scalding sensation, particularly when the urine comes in contact with them.

CAUSES.—Exposure to the virus of gonorrhœa, leucorrhœa, and menstrual secretions, want of cleanliness, errors in diet, excessive exercise, and a too frequent and violent coition may be set down as the chief causes of balanitis.

Men having an unusually long prepuce, and those troubled with congenital phymosis, are particularly prone to this complaint, and it is then caused by the accumulation and retardation of the follicular exudation, which becomes acrid and offensive, and ill adapted for the lubrication of so delicate a structure.

TREATMENT.—Strict cleanliness, frequent ablutions with tepid water and pure soap, the application of a pledget of lint between the abraded surface, first saturated with a solution of *Calendula, Carbolic acid, Tannic acid,* or the *Diacetate of lead,* as recommended by my friend Dr. Tuckey of Canterbury, with the administration of *Sepia* or *Mercurius,* will quickly remove the ordinary forms of balanitis. It will, however, sometimes assume an obstinate form, particularly when the cause is traceable to the virus emanating from a *gonorrhœa,* a *gleet,* a *chancroid,* or a *chancre.*

If from gonorrhœa, coupled with inflammatory symptoms, an occasional dose of *Aconite* or *Belladonna* should be prescribed, followed by *Cannabis, Merc. sol., Pulsatilla,* and *Sulphur.*

If from a gleet, *Corallium rubrum,* followed by *Sulphur.*

If from a soft sore, *Nitric acid* both internally and externally in a very weak solution has afforded me the best results.

If from a hard sore, one of the mercurial preparations should be selected, the *Merc. sol. Hah.* by
preference.

If from a soft sore, particularly when such sores
assume a corroding or serpiginous form, secreting a
fœtid humour, bleeding when touched, with sharp
stinging pains, I have in many cases witnessed the
most satisfactory results to follow the administration
of *nitric acid* in the first or second dilution ; with a
very weak solution of the same medicament, or the
calendula applied externally in the form of a lotion.

A balanitis when accompanied by a phymosis,
whether congenital or of recent origin, is perhaps one
of the most troublesome complications we have to
deal with; in such cases the discharge should be
removed by means of a series of syringefuls of tepid
water thrown up under the foreskin, followed by a
solution of *calendula, carbolic acid, tannic acid,* or black
wash, as suggested by Dr. Tuckey of Canterbury ;
this should be repeated twice or three times a day,
conjoined with soothing applications to the diseased
member, either cold or tepid, according to the temperament of the patient, until the inflammation and
pain shall have sufficiently subsided to enable us to
manipulate without giving pain or risk of danger.

In congenital phymosis a similar line of treatment
should be adopted ; and if a patient so formed should
be subjected to repeated attacks of a like kind, it
would become a matter for consideration whether a
surgical operation, either by dividing or circumcising
the foreskin, ought not to be performed—an operation
as simple as the results are, as a rule, satisfactory.

NOTE.—*Corallium rubrum* did good service in three cases of balanitis recently under my treatment, which would not yield kindly to other medicines,—two accompanied a clap, the third a gleet. The provings of red coral are striking and to the point, namely, "swelling of the prepuce, with a sore pain at the margin when touching it. Red flat ulcers on the glans and inner surface of the prepuce, with a quantity of yellow pus."

Attomyr, in his practical little work on venereal diseases records a case of balanitis accompanying a gleet cured by the same remedy. He says, "I treated two cases; one was accompanied with afterclap (gleet). The glans was red and swollen. It had slight fissures here and there, and one or two days afterwards it secreted some ill-smelling mucus, which in a short time increased very much, and drew the foreskin into sympathy. *Corallium* 3rd trituration, one grain, repeated after four days, cured the gonorrhœa of the gland," but *Cannabis sativa* and *Sulphur* cured the gleet.

The second case presented itself with chancre, was not so bad, and healed under the influence of mercury.

GONORRHŒA SYPALITICA—SYPHILITIC GONORRHŒA.

I have long considered it as an established fact, proved by the indubitable evidence of experience, that there are two kinds of contagious or vénereal gonorrhœa, one arising from the specific virus of clap—the seed organ, in fact, of "gonorrhœa;" the other the result of a true *syphilitic chancre*, situate in some part of the urethra; the former constituting a more or less local affection, yielding kindly enough to such well-proved remedies as *aconite, cannabis, cantharides, petroselinum, pulsatilla, sepia,* and *sulphur.*

The other, unless boldly and vigorously attacked by a well-selected preparation of *quicksilver,* the born enemy of the true "Hunterian sore," leaves in its train a motley and hideous group of phenomena, which is characteristic of the true *syphilitic* type.

This is a form of gonorrhœa the real cause of which is too frequently overlooked by many medical men, whilst the obstinacy of the complaint—"discharge," which goes on perhaps for months, in spite of the most judiciously selected gonorrhœal specifics, and the most powerful injections—is too frequently attributed more to a peculiar idiosyncrasy of constitution, than to the treacherous *chancre* that lays nestling, as it were, within the folds of the mucus membrane of the urethra.

The leading symptoms of this form of gonorrhœa

should hold a prominent place in the memory of those who undertake the treatment of such disorders. True, there is a certain bluntness and obscurity, "if I may so term it," in some of the most prominent phenomena ; but that very obscurity should lead the mind to con-jecture that there *may* be something more in the urethra than a trifling clap or an obstinate gleet.

In carefully noting the symptoms of a patient so afflicted, he will invariably tell you that he has suffered but little inflammation even from the very outset of the complaint—that he has suffered but little pain—that he has scarcely had any scalding in passing his water, and that the discharge has been going on steadily from day to day and week to week, in defiance of all the medicines he may have taken, and all the injections he may have thrown into the urethra.

A careful examination of the lips of the urethra—the corona glandis and reflections of the prepuce—will frequently reveal concealed under a thickish deposit of *balanitis*, not only erosions and *figwarts*, but a real chancre as well ; but if not found here, and not satis-fied with such a diagnosis, trace carefully with the fingers of both hands the course of the penis from the tip to its root, and you will find somewhere about midway a hard cartilaginous substance which will not yield to pressure, or gives but little pain ; this is the "fons et origo mali."

There is another landmark connected with this form of gonorrhœa which I wish to direct the attention of my readers to ; it has, however, not failed me in diagnosing twenty-five cases of a like kind which have come under my observation ; namely, a peculiar puckering and drawing in, as it were, of the lips of the urethra, which always reminds me of the same phenomena observed in case of scirrhus of the breast. This symptom was very prominently marked in an exceedingly interesting case which came under my notice some months ago. The patient, a man of fifty years old, had contracted what he was led to believe was an ordinary attack of gonorrhœa, and was treated as such by four different medical men. Deriving no benefit from these gentlemen, he applied for advice at one of the London Lock Hospitals. I saw this patient on his first visit, listened to the history of his case, and watched the progress of the treatment till an excellent cure was effected. There was distinctly marked the peculiar puckering and *inversion* of the lips of the urethra, as if drawn by some power from within; there was the constant weeping of matter, unattended by any particular pain or ardor; about an inch or so below the orifice of the urethra was diagnosed a hard, firm, unyielding body, about the size of a small filbert, which seemed to encircle the canal like a ring, unattended by any marked tenderness or pain. The age and sallow look of this man; the size and cartilaginous feel of the tumour, coupled with other circumstances, raised suspicions in the minds of the medical officers in attendance that the disease was of a malignant type. Amputation was suggested, but happily deferred, and he was placed — as an experiment—under a course of mercury, according to the ordinary formula in use at that institution. In fourteen days the substance, "which I shall now designate as chancre," was reduced to half its original size. In twenty-eight days there was a further reduction; and in eight weeks every vestige had disappeared, *and* an excellent cure was effected.

GONORRHŒA VIRULENTA.

Of all the varied forms of venereal disease there
are none, it may safely be affirmed, that inflict so much
torture and acute suffering on the patient than a well-
developed case of gonorrhœa, which may be defined
" as *a specific inflammation* of an acute form affecting
the mucous surface of the urinary and sexual passages
in both sexes; followed by a copious puriform or
muco-purulent, sanguineous discharge, propagated by
contact, and in some instances occasioning severe
and dangerous consequences."

To the medical practitioner, also, a gonorrhœa will
sometimes prove an obstinate and troublesome complaint to deal with. This I attribute partly to its *metastatic* propensities, and partly on account of its tendency
to assume a chronic form, under the epithet afterclap,
or gleet. To the peculiar idosyncrasies of constitutions; to the daily pursuits of some, the habits and
mode of living of others; to the restricted calibre of
the urethral canal, coupled with the naturally indolent
character of the mucous membranes, must undoubtedly
be attributed this unsatisfactory and uncertain state of
things. Thus we may frequently perceive that *catarrhs*,
which often in themselves and *per se* are unimportant,
will continue for several weeks and even months; and
the same may be observed in various affections of the
mucous membrane of the *bronchi*, the *nose, ears, vagina*,
and *rectum*, which often become more protracted in

D

their duration in proportion to the increase of the
secretion of mucus.

SYMPTOMS.—An ordinary attack of gonorrhœa
runs a somewhat similar course to an ordinary attack
of inflammation, namely, the stage of irritation or
congestion ; the stage of inflammation ; thirdly, the
stage of suppuration ; terminating, fourthly, in the
stage of decline, or a gleet.

1. THE STAGE OF CONGESTION.—After a period
of incubation varying from two to five or six
days there is experienced a slight itching or tingling at the orifice of the urethra, the lips of which
are slightly tumid, accompanied by a slight smarting
sensation in passing water, and a trifling discharge of
a thin transparent mucus, or a milk-and-water-like
fluid, which after two or three days reveals under the
field of the microscope mucus and pus globules. To
this succeeds the—

2. INFLAMMATORY STAGE, which is characterized by an intensely painful, highly sensitive,
and cord-like touch of the penis ; an increased puffi-
ness of the urethral lips ; excoriation, and a peculiar
cherry-like colour of the glans ; a burning, scalding sensation in passing water, which is diminished
in quantity, and comes away either in drops, or in a
curling, broken, or twisted stream ; with a copious discharge of a thick yellow purulent or sanguineous greenish matter. In some cases, particularly in first claps,
occurring in young robust and inflammatory persons,
the inflammation and swelling of the penis is so intense
as to lead for some hours to a complete retention of
urine, and the extension of the pain along the whole

course of the urethra to the bladder, the perinæum
the hypogastric region, and even down to the hips and
thighs ; and so intense a nature do these symptoms
sometimes assume, that the discharge is almost suppressed, constituting that form of the complaint designated "*gonorrhœa sicca,*" dry gonorrhœa. This stage
may continue with more or less severity for seven, ten,
or fourteen days, when the more prominent symptoms
will gradually subside ; the discharge diminishes in
quantity and purulency, and the pain and scalding
become less intense ; and at the expiration of from
three to six weeks all traces of the disease may disappear. I have, however, met with many cases of
gonorrhœa which have entirely disappeared in twelve,
fifteen, and twenty days, particularly in those who
have sought early advice, and were blessed with a good
constitution and contented mind ; who were likewise
in a position to lay up, and carry out strictly the
dietetic, hygienic, and *therapeutic* rules set down for
their guidance.

Sometimes, however, although the acute symptoms
shall have subsided, and the discharge considerably
lessened and altered in quality, the urethra, instead
of resuming its natural healthy mucous secretion, will
persist in pouring out from time to time for an in-
definite period a thin, glairy milk and water, or light
green coloured matter, constituting what I am disposed to designate the fourth stage of the complaint,
known as a "gleet," or afterclap.

Such, then, is a brief outline of the course and
various stages of an ordinary attack of gonorrhœa,
and 'twere well, both for patient and physician, if it

never deviated from that course, "painful though
some of the symptoms might be." This, however, is
not the case. A gonorrhœa is at best, and under the
most favourable circumstances, a capricious and
whimsical disorder to deal with : one case will run an
even and unchequered course to convalescence, and
totally disappear in the course of fifteen to twenty
days; whilst another, in spite of the most careful
nursing, the strictest diet, and the most judiciously
selected medicines, will assume an obstinate and aggravated form from the very commencement of the
attack, by developing some of its most serious and
painful complications, which hang on and torture the
patient for weeks and months.

In ordinary cases of gonorrhœa the inflammation
does not extend further along the urethra than an inch
and a half or two inches from the orifice—the *specific
extent* of John Hunter ; but in severe forms of the
complaint the inflammation passes along the whole
course of the urethra, and even implicates the mucous
membrane of the bladder as well. It deposits fibrine
in the *corpora spongiosa urethræ*, the exciting cause
of that very painful complication, *chordee*. It invades
the prepuce, which becomes thickened, swollen, excoriated, and œdematous, producing that condition
termed phimosis. It extends to the inguinal region
and descends into the scrotum ; hence those painfully
sympathetic buboes in the groins, and inflammatory
enlargement of the testicles. In its course along the
urethra towards the bladder it invades the *prostate*
and *Cowper's* glands, creating a most painful and dangerous form of inflammation, which either terminates

in suppuration, or chronic enlargement, coupled with the most distressing form of *dysuria*.

For a more concise description of the symptoms and treatment of these disorders the reader is referred to that section of the work which treats of the " Complications of Gonorrhœa," page 48.

CAUSES.—Many and varied are the causes capable of inducing an inflammation of the urethra, which may terminate in a gonorrhœal discharge, and which need not necessarily be the result of an *impure embrace ;* amongst these I would briefly mention—

1. MECHANICAL CAUSES—such as the introduction of a catheter or bougie, the passage of calculi, or the introduction of other foreign bodies into the urethra.

2. CHEMICAL CAUSES—such as the injection of irritating substances, abuse of spirits, new wine, unfermented beer, stimulating spices, and salt food.

3. CLIMATIC CAUSES. — It is considered that gonorrhœa occurs more frequently in a hot than a cold climate, and it has been observed that exposure of the organs to the wind while urinating* is a frequent cause of a discharge from the urethra, which runs the same course as an ordinary attack of gonorrhœa.

4. CONSTITUTIONAL CAUSES.—The forms of constitutional irritation which predispose one more particularly to gonorrhœa are *scrofula, tubercles, gout, rheumatism, piles,* and various *cutaneous eruptions ;* and as regards predisposition or temperament it may

---

* This I have observed among the farm labourers and shepherds of the Welsh mountains, who take the Petroselinum, or Parsley-root tea, as a remedy—a remedy of great antiquity.

be noted that persons of a plethoric habit, with blond hair, a fine white colour, and delicate frame, or those whose constitutions savour of the sanguine or scrofulous taint, are more liable to be infected, and have it· in a more severe form than those who do not possess those qualities.

5. MASTURBATION.—I have occasionally observed that some of those young men who seek my advice for the ill-effects produced by that *deplorable* and *pernicious vice*, self-pollution or onanism, are subject to a gleety discharge from the urethra. This was well marked in the case of a youth of sixteen, who was brought to me from a large seminary at Blackheath some few days since, the discovery of which was the means of checking a habit which had obtained a firm hold upon many of his confrères as well.

FINALLY, a gonorrhœal discharge may be induced by excessive sexual intercourse, by *leucorrhœa*, by ulceration of the neck of the womb, and by having intercourse with women during the *menstrual period*. I have occasionally met with cases of the latter kind which have really been the cause of a very sharp attack of the complaint, and have particularly noticed the pain to be of a peculiarly *stinging* character. This form of gonorrhœa did not escape the observation of the ancient physicians, as John of Gadisden, M.D., Merton College, Oxford, in his *Rosa Anglica*, 1320, refers to the "menstrual flux" as a cause of gonorrhœa; while similar observations are to be found in other works extending from that period to the present day. But the most frequent cause of *gonorrhœa*, and the one we are more· immediately interested in at the present time, is that which springs from a "specific virus," communicable to a healthy person by an *impure coit*, or by inoculation.

Of the nature, character, and chemical properties of this *virus* we know no more than we do of the poison of the *viper*, the *rattlesnake*, or the *spear-headed serpent* of South America ; its effects on the healthy organism are, however, tangible enough, and form a group of morbid phenomena so prominent and graphic that, once seen or felt, can never be forgotten, and present an apt *simile* to the burnt child who never forgets the element that inflicted upon him so much suffering.

To the treatment of gonorrhœa I would now direct attention.

It is an exceedingly interesting study, and one peculiarly fitted to convince the opponents of homœopathy of the beauty and simplicity of its guiding principle, *similia similibus curantur*, and the efficacy of drugs administered, comparatively speaking, in inappreciable doses. This treatment we shall divide into PREVENTIVE and CURATIVE.

1. The PREVENTIVE or prophylactic treatment I adopt on the same principle as we do the administration of *Belladonna* in scarlet fever, *Pulsatilla* in measles, *Quinine* in intermittent fever, and vaccination against small-pox, &c. A gonorrhœa, " like many febrile and eruptive diseases," has its stage of *incubation*, the duration of which varies, according to Druitt, from four to five days, but may extend, according to Cooper, to *two* and even *three* weeks. It is during this stage that a well-selected PREVENTIVE should be

administered, and of sufficient potency to create in the organism a group of syptoms *similar* to those produced by the virus of gonorrhœa, particularly in the mucous membrane of the urethra. We have in *Mercury* such a remedy ; at all events, let us compare notes, and see how near it approaches in its homœopathicity to that disease.

MERCURY causes a burning and smarting in the urethra.

It causes a frequent desire to urinate.

It causes blood to pass with the water.

It causes shreds and flocks of white mucus to pass with the water.

It causes a burning, cutting, prickling pain in passing water.

It causes a cutting, biting pain all along the urethra, especially at the orifice during the emission of the last few drops of water.

It causes itching of the glans, prepuce, and orifice of the urethra.

It causes inflammation and œdematous swelling of the prepuce, as if filled with water.

It causes swelling of the penis, especially at night, often accompanied with painful erections.

It causes *condylomata* on the prepuce, and the exudation of pus from the urethra and behind the "*corona glandis.*"

In the female also *Mercury* acts with considerable energy.

It causes an inflammatory swelling of the vaginal mucous membrane, with a feeling as if the parts were raw and excoriated ; a discharge of flocks of mucus and pus from the vagina ; it likewise causes a purulent, corrosive leucorrhœa.

The general symptoms also "produced by this drug" bear a strong resemblance to the first impression made upon the system by the contagious virus, and before the appearance of any local symptoms ; namely,—*depression of strength, præcordial anxiety, frequent sighing, a sense of coldness, partial or general tremors, an anxious or pinched countenance, and a small quick pulse.* These symptoms, which so fully point out its *primary* action on the nervous system, are frequently felt by sensitive and observant patients about to suffer from an attack of gonorrhœa; and if there be any truth in the homœopathic law, and any reliance to be placed on the *preventive* power of any drug, I know of no medicine so closely allied in its homœopathicity, or so certain in its effects, as one of the mercurial preparations, more particularly the *Merc. vivus* or the *Merc. sol. Hah.*

Dr. Croserio, of Paris, had unbounded faith in the preventive power of these preparations ; indeed, he never found them fail, provided his instructions were strictly carried out. His favourite potency was the 30th—a dose every night during three or four days.

Whenever a patient consults me who has been exposed to a doubtful contact, I invariably lay down the following simple rules :—

A. That he should live plainly, avoid all stimulants and unnecessary excitement.

B. That he should immediately wash the parts with tepid water and pure soap ; to which may be added carbolic acid, or Condy's fluid.

C. That the urine should be quickly voided, using more than ordinary force in doing so, because by this means the morbid matter which might have adhered to thelips of the urethra may be expelled or carried away with the rush of water ; and—

D. That he should take *Merc. sol. Hah.* 3x or 6x night and morning for some days.

2. CURATIVE TREATMENT.—In the incipient or congestive stage of gonorrhœa, when the patient simply complains of a *tingling, titillating* sensation at the orifice of the urethra ; a slight redness and pouting of its lips, with no perceptible discharge beyond a thin glairy, albuminous-looking mucus, and barely sufficient to close the orifice of the urethra by agglutination, I generally prescribe *Sepia* 6, a dose three times a day, which has in some cases cut short the further progress of the complaint, and in others has had a very modifying effect on the inflammatory stage.

SEPIA fairly covers these symptoms. It produces a *tingling, titillating,* or *smarting* sensation in the urethra during micturition, itching of the prepuce, and a discharge of a *milky fluid.* It is not often, however, that the physician has an opportunity of treating the disorder at so early a stage, as the generality of such patients are too prone to delay seeking advice till it reaches that condition sometimes described as a *roaring clap.* This may be attributed to various causes. *Syphilitic* and *venereal* patients, with few exceptions, are young and single men, who live at home with their friends and relatives ; at a boarding-house, an hotel, or with their employers ; consequently, feel a delicacy in communicating to those around them the filthy nature of the disease contracted, and the fix they have got into ; and, in order to avoid suspicion, make no alteration in their pursuits or mode of living, and thus allow the disease to go on from stage to stage, until they can bear it no longer. Some will treat a gonorrhœa as they would a cold, and do a little domestic prescribing ; some will, with a false economy, seek the advice of some ignorant chemist : if *allopathic*, he is well drenched with copaiva and cubebs ; and, if *homœopathic*, is badly doctored under the guidance of some tinkering "domestic," concocted and strung together by some penny-a-liner. It is thus found that a considerable number of persons so afflicted do not seek proper advice until the complaint has made rapid and destructive inroads on the constitution, and, in many cases, laid the foundation of *incurable disorders*.

In the inflammatory stage *Aconite, Cannabis sativa,* and *Merc. sol.* step in as admirable remedies, conjoined with perfect rest, a bland diet, copious draughts of cold water, barley water, gum water, or linseed tea ; the frequent ablution of the penis with tepid water and soap, and the constant application of compresses saturated with either cold or tepid water. It is seldom I have had occasion to vary these remedies except it be in those concomitant symptoms described under the head of " Complications of Gonorrhœa." *Aconite* will calm the nervous system, subdue fever, and considerably modify that painful and anxious urging to urinate ; that difficult and scanty emission of hot, scalding urine ; that burning and tenesmus

which sometimes extends to the neck of the bladder;
that itchingof the prepuce, and that piercing and
pinching in the glands on urinating, often met with
in this stage.   It should be administered in drop
doses of the tincture, or a pilule of the second or
third decimal dilution every one or two hours, till the
more urgent symptoms are subdued.

. *Cannabis sativa* ranks high, and deservedly so, as
a curative agent in the acute form of gonorrhœa ; it
is a medicine which has met with general approval
from those who have paid anything like ordinary
attention to that class of diseases designated *venereal.*

Its pathogenetic effects on the urinary organs are
remarkably striking, and form as true a picture of the
complaint as any drug I know of. Thus we find it
develops a *burning, smarting, darting, stitching,*
tearing pain in the urethra, which extends from its
orifice, as far back as the bladder, producing a form
of CYSTITIS.

It develops a discharge of pus from the urethra ; a
sensation of tearing in the fibres of the canal, with a
smarting, stinging pain during micturition. It develops strangury, with painful discharge of drops of
bloody urine.   It develops a swelling of the prostate gland ; a swollen condition of the penis, glans,
and prepuce ; with a corrosive burning and stinging
of the preputial margin ; and it creates a tensive
pain in the spermatic cord, contraction of the
scrotum, with a sense of pressure, and dragging of
the testicles ; thus completing, as it were, a picture of
gonorrhœa.

With regard to the best potency and repetition

of the dose, differences of opinion exist. Many
physicians give several drops of the mother tincture
night and morning, but Hahnemann laid it down
as a rule that the high dynamizations, and even
the very highest, develop the medicinal virtues of
this plant to a much greater degree ; so that during
the latter years of his life he always gave it in the
30th dilution, dissolved successively in two glasses
of water. Drs. Croserio, Hartmann, and Gross followed the example of our master, the latter de-
claring that with a single dose of the 200th he
succeeded much better than with repeated doses of
the mother tincture. Jahr recommends the 3rd,
Attomyr the 4th, repeated every fourth or fifth day,
and invariably cured his patients in one month,
some in fourteen days. Hempel varies his potencies
from the matrix upwards, and quotes a case
" where chordee was a very prominent and painful
symptom," which he cured in fourteen days by means
of large doses of the tincture, commencing with five
drops the first day, and gradually increasing it to
thirty drops in the course of the twenty-four hours.

Yeldham, in his sensational little brochure on Venereal Diseases, in terms not very complimentary to the
memory of Hahnemann, or the experience of those eminent men just mentioned, dogmatically states that *to do
good, Cannabis* must be given in *palpable* doses. " I am,"
he says, " in the habit of prescribing from five to ten, or
even fifteen drops of the mother tincture three or
four times a day. In my own practice," he further
observes, " the dilutions have proved *nearly* if not *quite
inert.*" A somewhat considerable experience during

the last twenty years enables me to refute such statements, and confirm the views set down by the revered
master of our doctrine and his early disciples, as I
have over and over again witnessed the most favourable results to follow the administration of *Cannabis* in
potencies varying from the *first* to the *thirtieth* dilution,
selected with due regard to the temperament and
constitution of my patients.

Merc. sol. Hah. ranks next in importance as a
curative agent in the acute form of gonorrhœa ;
indeed, a careful study of its pathogenesy gives it
even a closer homœopathicity to the disease than
the preceding remedy.   I generally select it when the
local inflammatory symptoms run high, either from
neglect of the patient, or from previous bad treatment ;
when the discharge is green and bloody, with painful
erections and a swollen prepuce.

Here are its pathogenetic effects on the urethra :—
Constant desire to urinate.

The urine looks as if mixed with pus or mucus.

Burning in the urethra between the   acts   of
micturition.

Discharge of blood from the urethra.

Cutting pains in the urethra, and a

Greenish gonorrhœal discharge from the urethra.

On the genital organs we find the following :—

Inflammation of the prepuce, with burning
pain.

Swelling of the prepuce, as if distended into a blis-
ter with water or air.

Inflammatory redness on the internal surface of
the prepuce, with great sensitiveness to pain.

Swelling of the anterior part of the urethra, with suppuration between the prepuce and glans.

Drawing pains in the testicles, extending into the groin.

Drawing in the spermatic cord.

Hard swelling of the testicles, with shining redness of the scrotum.

Painful erections, &c.

Potency and repetition of the dose. Hahnemann never used the medicines lower than the 30th dilution. Croserio the same, and when febrile symptoms ran high, he gave one dose of *Aconite ;* then *Merc.* every second or third day, according to circumstances; and as soon as an evident amelioration took place all medicine was suspended. Gross declared that a single dose of the 200th was sufficient to cure the disease, if permitted to act a suitable time. Attomyr selected the 4th when he found the discharge of a greenish colour and attended with ulcers,—" what kind of ulcers he does not say."

Thuja is another remedy I am disposed to class with the foregoing ; it bears a strong resemblance in its mode of action to *Cannabis sativa,* and has done good service in many cases where that remedy was indicated, particularly when attended by warts—a phimosis or paraphimosis. In the female I invariably select it in preference to any other, and vary the potency from the 1st to the 3rd dilution.

COMPLICATIONS OF GONORRHŒA.

Following in the wake of the inflammatory stage of gonorrhœa, we sometimes encounter a series of concomitant symptoms, some of a mild form, others of a very painful and distressing nature. Amongst these I would mention—

1. That long-continued and very painful erection of the penis familiarly known as a CHORDEE. John Hunter recognised two forms of it, the *inflammatory* and *spasmodic*. The first arises from a deposit of lymph in the *corpus spongiosum urethra*, which glues together the cells, and prevents their distension, so that when the penis is full of blood it is bent forward "crescentic-like," with its concavity looking downwards. The second comes and goes at no fixed periods ; at one time there will be an erection, entirely free from pain or curvature; at another the pain will be severely felt ; and this will frequently recur at varied and sometimes short intervals. *Cantharis, Capsicum,* or *Pulsatilla,* exercises a marked influence over the former, conjoined with the application of cold compresses to the penis, the use of cold hip baths, one or more Turkish baths, a plain and moderately low diet, such as boiled cod, sole, or tripe, diluent drinks, and no stronger stimulant than a wine-glassful of Hungarian Somlau, diffused in one-half to a tumblerful of distilled water, or better still, copious draughts of barley water or linseed tea.

In the spasmodic form, *Nux vomica* and *Camphor*, both internally and externally, have yielded me the most satisfactory results.

2. HÆMORRHAGE.—Bleeding from the urethra is not an uncommon symptom of an acute attack of gonorrhœa, and arises from a rupture of some of the over-distended capillaries during a violent and pain ful erection, or that condition termed *chordee*. A moderate loss of blood may act as a palliative by relieving the over-gorged blood-vessels, subduing inflammation, and thus modifying the severity of the chordee, consequently should not be checked ; but an excessive loss of blood should be arrested by placing the patient in the horizontal posture, the application of cold compresses, and the administration of such remedies as *Aconite, Nitric acid, Cantharides,* or *Hamamelis.*

3. PHIMOSIS, which signifies a muzzle, is another painful attendant on acute gonorrhœa, frequently caused by and consequently closely allied to the last-named condition.   It consists of an inflammation of the prepuce, which becomes thickened, puffy, and swollen, and so constricted as to render it a frequent impossibility to uncover the glans.

The treatment should consist of cold water compresses ; the removal of all discharge from underneath the prepuce by means of a syringe and tepid water, to which may be added carbolic acid or Condy's fluid, and the administration of *Merc. sol., Thuja,* and sometimes *Cannabis.* This sometimes terminates in—

4. PARAPHIMOSIS, which signifies a bridle,—the

E

circumligatura of Galen, or the strangulating phimosis of Good. It consists of a constricted condition of the prepuce behind the glans, which cannot be brought forward again. If the constriction is not speedily removed the inflammation soon reaches a dangerous height, and invades the whole penis.

The treatment here should be prompt and decisive, our first step being to reduce the glans to as small a size as possible: this may be accomplished by first applying cold lotions, ice, or ice water, and then compressing the glans equally and unremittingly for some minutes between the fingers and thumbs of both hands, and when as much blood as practicable is pressed out, and the organ is reduced to its smallest size, we should then press it back with the thumbs through the constricted prepuce, while the fingers at the same time are used in coaxing the prepuce forward over the glans. Should these means however fail, which is seldom the case, and the constriction be such as to threaten to terminate in more serious mischief, such as ulceration and sloughing of the parts, no time should be lost in dividing the constriction by means of a sharp-pointed, narrow-curved bistoury. The stricture will invariably be found behind the crown of the glans, and separated from it by a raised ring, consisting of a swollen portion of the prepuce, thus forming for itself a kind of depression or groove ; into this groove the point of the knife should be passed deeply enough to go under the stricture, which may then be divided by cutting upwards. The member should then be wrapped in lint or soft linen, first saturated in a weak solution of *Arnica* or

Calendula, either tepid or cold, according to the temperament of the patient ; and the administration of either *Cannabis, Sativa, Merc. sol.,* or *Sabina.*

5. PROSTATITIS.—Acute inflammation of the prostate gland will sometimes arrest our attention, as a prominent and painful complication of a gonorrhœa, and is most frequently met with in those cases which occur in irritable and scrofulous constitutions. The symptoms, as a rule, are well marked : there is a sensation of pressure and heat in that part of the *perinæum* which is in close contiguity to the neck of the bladder and rectum, with a painful and almost constant desire to evacuate the contents of those organs ; there is a sensation as if a foreign body were lodged. in the rectum, with a correspondingly outward swelling, easily diagnosed by external manipulation or an internal exploration, the parts as a rule being highly sensitive and painful on pressure. It may terminate in one of three different ways ; namely, *resolution, suppuration,* or *chronic enlargement,* of which the last may prove a very troublesome companion to the patient during the remainder of his days. The treatment here also should be prompt and decisive. The recumbent posture becomes a *sine quâ non.* All stimulating substances should be strictly prohibited, and cold evaporating lotions should be kept constantly applied to the perinæum, prepared according to the following formula :—

Liquor Plumbi. Diacetatis. ʒij.

spr. Vin. Rect. ℥ij.

Aqua puræ ℥xiv. Misce.

Fiat Lotio.

Bland diluent drinks only should be allowed, such as gum water, barley water, or linseed tea, and the administration of *Aconite* second decimal, or *Belladonna* in drop doses every one or two hours. *Merc. sol.* and *Pulsatilla* should not be forgotten, as they chime in as excellent remedies, either alone or in alternation with either of the foregoing, more particularly the latter, as it offers in its SYMPTOMOLOGICAL EFFECTS, the largest number of symptoms which accord to this disease. The action of the selected medicine should be rigidly administered, and carefully watched until a change takes place for better or worse. If the former, there will be observed a gradual cessation of pain, a more prolonged desire, with less pain and difficulty to pass water, a diminution in the size of the swelling, and a more uniform ease and comfort will pervade the whole frame ; in fact, its terminating in the most favourable form, namely, *resolution*. Should, however, suppuration, " in spite of these remedies," take place, we then have, as indices, general rigors, a dull throbbing pain, with a sensation of weight, and obscure swelling of a doughy feel in the perinæum ; this should be hastened to maturity in the shortest possible time, and I know of no medicines better adapted for that purpose than *Hep. sulph.* and *Silicea.* A repetition of either of these remedies every two to four hours, for twenty to thirty hours, will bring the abscess to a point, so as to enable the surgeon to operate without risk, which should at once be done, by making a free puncture with a sharp-pointed bistoury. This form of abscess, if left to take its own course, may burst into the rectum or urethra, or into the cellular tissue of the perinæum, and cause considerable constitutional disturbance, and sometimes irreparable mischief, which may terminate in death.

In chronic enlargement of the prostate gland I have found great benefit to follow the administration of *Merc. bin-iod.*, *Kali hydriodicum*, with an occasional dose of *Sulphur*.

6. DYSURIA.—Irritation, and sometimes inflammation, of the mucous membrane of the bladder, is another occasional symptom of a severe clap. It is attended with extreme suffering and annoyance, the bladder at times becoming so irritable that the retention of the smallest quantity of urine puts the patient to the most intolerable anguish. In addition to these symptoms we have generally considerable fever, a quick pulse, with listless, sleepless, and distressing nights. A perpetual tenesmus is also present, which creates a constant desire to evacuate the contents of that viscus, which comes away in small quantities, causing a burning, scalding sensation, which reaches its climax while passing the last few drops. The urine is generally turbid, and highly charged with *mucus, blood,* and *pus.*

TREATMENT.—The principal remedies for this very painful and distressing form of the complaint are undoubtedly *Aconite* and *Cantharides*, which may be administered alternately every half to one hour, until the more acute symptoms shall have subsided ; the medicine may then be administered at longer intervals, and, if all feverish symptoms have subsided, *Acon.* may be omitted, and *Canth.* given a little longer.   In the more chronic form *Merc. sol.* and *Nux vom.* step in as very useful remedies ; *Merc.* when the urine is turbid, fœtid, and charged with thick, flocky mucus ; *Nux vom.* when there exists a peculiar irritation at the neck of the bladder, causing a frequent desire to urinate, gastric and hepatic derangement, with constipation and hæmorr-hoidal affections.   A diet of the blandest kind, hip baths, warm applications to the perinæum and anal region, in the form of linseed meal or bran poultices, with gum water, barley water, or linseed tea as beverages, constitute the dietetic and hygienic rules which I am in the habit of adopting.

7. BUBOES.—Inflammation and enlargement of the inguinal glands constitute another painful attend-ant on a gonorrhœa, and may be set down as one of the *metastatic* forms of the complaint; they, how-ever, seldom suppurate, and generally appear in persons infected for the first time, whose constitutions savour of the sanguine or scrofulous taint, and who too frequently, from the commencement, treat a clap as a trifle, by indulging in walking, dancing, riding, and cricketing, with no small amount of high living. I have met with many cases arising from each of those causes ; in some the glands assumed an enormous size, were exceedingly painful, and slow in dispersing. These glandular swellings supervene in about the first twelve or fourteen days of a gonorrhœa, that is, while it runs through its inflammatory stage, and is caused by the pus being absorbed by the lymphatic vessels of the penis, which carry it into the groin, and there set up an inflammatory action, which will in

some cases run through its regular stages to suppuration.

In the treatment of this type of bubo we must
in a great measure be guided by the stage and condition of the gonorrhœa ; remove this, the other follows ; strike at the root, the branches fall and wither.

Should it result from a sudden suppression of the
gonorrhœal discharge, which may follow the use of
astringent injections, or exposure to wet and cold,
the re-establishment of the discharge should be our
first object.   This I have succeeded in accomplishing
with *Pulsatilla* in the majority of cases, and with
Sulphur in others, where the former had failed.
These cases were afterwards cured by *Cannabis*,
Sativa, *Merc. bin-iod.*, *Kali*, and *Sulphur*.

The buboes, if very painful, hard, and tense, should
be treated with cold evaporating lotions, and perfect
rest in the semi-recumbent posture ; but should this
fail, and there is followed an increased redness, a feeling of fluctuation which would lead us to infer that
pus had formed, we should then treat the case as a
common abscess, and hasten the suppurative process
by the help of *Hep. sulph.* or *Silicea*, and the application of warm poultices till the abscess is *ripe* for
opening, which I am in the habit of doing with a
curved, sharp-pointed bistoury, carried from above
downwards in a straight line.

8. ORCHITIS, or EPIDIDYMITIS BLENORRHAGICA,
absurdly set down as " hernia humoralis " by the old
writers.—Acute inflammation of the epididymis con-
stitutes one of the most frequent, painful, and dangerous of the metastatic concomitants of gonorrhœa ;

it not only produces irritation and inflammation of a severe and alarming nature, but sometimes terminates in abscess, extensive sloughing, in hydrocele, and in hypertrophy, with more or less deterioration in the functions of these organs. A swollen testicle may arise from various causes, such as the injection of irritating lotions, the passage of instruments, the lodgment of calculi, a blow, exposure to cold, or violent exercise ; but the form we are now more particularly interested in, is that which takes place as the result of a suppressed gonorrhœa, terminating in *metastasis*—literally, the transfer of a disease from one organ of the body to another.

The symptoms are prominent and unmistakable. About a fortnight more or less after contracting a clap, the patient observes a partial or complete cessation of the urethral discharge, followed by a sensation of weight, fulness, and tenderness in the spermatic cord. When the case is further advanced, the swelling extends to the whole of the testicle, which becomes so swollen that the scrotum loses its natural corrugated appearance, and becomes tense, smooth, shining, and reddened, and sometimes of a purplish hue. The pain now is of the most excruciating kind, and extends to the lumbar and inguinal regions, as well as the hips and thighs. Serious constitutional symptoms now set in, in the form of a small, quick, jerking pulse ; a hard, stunning headache ; great restlessness, thirst, a furred tongue, loss of appetite ; a hard, dry skin ; obstinate constipation ; and, in some cases, vomiting, with other symptoms of inflammatory fever.

In the treatment of swollen testicles, we have in *Acon., Bell., Aur. met., Clematis, Merc. sol., Puls.,* and *Sulphur,* brilliant remedies.   On the first indication of inflammatory symptoms the patient should seek the recumbent posture ; avoid all highly seasoned food and stimulating drinks ; he should, in fact, restrict himself to almost fever diet ; and he should take a warm bath every second or third day.   The testes should be well supported, or allowed to rest on a small pillow placed between the thighs, and a lotion consisting of Tr. Aconite, ʒij, Rectified Spirit, ʒij, to sixteen ounces of water, should be kept constantly applied to the affected parts by means of a linen compress or lint.   *Aconite,* second dec., a drop or two in water should be administered and repeated at intervals of two hours for the first day.   It will not cure the TESTITIS but it will go far to help us in calming the nervous system, in toning down that restlessness, in blunting that terrific *stunning* headache which I have seldom missed, and deem almost *pathognomonic* of the complaint ; in moderating the heart's action, in substituting for that hard, dry skin a soothing glow and dewy perspiration, and in rendering the system more susceptible to the action of its specific.

The *Anemone pratensis,* or little Pasque-flower, is, however, a valiant remedy, and slays its victims with unerring aim, and the power of a Samson.   Its virtues have been lauded, and its praises have been sung by Hahnemann, Croserio, Jahr, Hempel, and many more, as an almost infallible specific.   Twenty-four cases of the acute inflammatory form, as recorded in my casebooks during the last three years, yielded quickly to

Pulsatilla, with the help of an occasional dose of *Acon.* or *Bell.* In the majority of those cases the scrotal symptoms were traced to the too early use of injections, exposure to cold and wet, and irregularity in diet.

Here are its leading SYMPTOMOLOGICAL EFFECTS on the genital organs in man :—Swelling of the right spermatic cord and testicles, with a tensive pain ; drawing tensive pains pass out of the abdomen through the spermatic cord into the testicles, the testes and spermatic cords are painful and swollen with discharge of fluid ; swelling of the scrotum with lacerating pains in the testes. The potency I vary from the 2nd to the 6th decimal dilution repeated every third or fourth hour, and when the inflammation assumes a phlegmonous form I alternate it with *Belladonna* third dilution.

The *Clematis Erecta* is another medicine which has done me good service in twenty cases of orchitis, the symptoms of which indicated the use of that drug, namely, *a bruised painful feeling of the testes* on being touched ; *a drawing pain in these bodies and spermatic cord from below upwards*, with a *frequent sexual desire.* The last of this group of cases came under my notice in January, 1876, which I will briefly record. J. P., æt. 47, married, an elastic brace manufacturer, consulted me January 17, 1876. Notes.—Contracted a clap three weeks since, for which he treated himself with salines and Sulphate of Zinc injections. There is scarcely any discharge per urethra, but there is considerable swelling of left testicle, the scrotum is tense and of a bluish red ; he is feverish, has rigors, alternating with heats ; the tongue is coated with a brownish mucous deposit ;

there is a dragging pain in the lumbar region, which extends to the hips, groins, and thighs ; the bowels are costive, urine thick and scanty, and there is a peculiar drawing up of the testicle and spermatic cord, with a frequent desire for venery.—*Clematis* 6th dec. every two or three hours.

January 20.—The testicles are smaller and less painful, but he continues feverish : to take *Acon.* 2 at bedtime and *Clematis* every four hours.

January 22.—There is considerable improvement, the feverish symptoms have subsided ; the swelling and pain is considerably diminished ; there is an increased discharge per urethra ; urine more copious, and the bowels have been moved freely by the aid of a Seidlitz powder. To continue the *Clematis.*

January 25.—The testicles are reduced to their normal size and free from pain; has an increased discharge, but no heat or scalding ; he, however, complains of a sudden and frequent desire to make water, a symptom I covered with *Sulphur* 6, which removed every vestige of the disorder in the course of another seven days.

Dr. Hirschel regards the *Clematis* as a valuable agent when orchitis supervenes on exposure to cold after a gonorrhœa ; the testicle becoming indurated, sensitive to pressure ; the scrotum red, swollen, with tearing, drawing pains, " *and retraction of the testicles and spermatic cord,*"—the chief indication for the selection of that medicine. Ruckert, Marcy, and Hunt speak favourably of it, and record some interesting cases of the kind. Attomyr also is not silent on the same subject, a she records two cases of swollen testicles : one was cured by *Clematis* and

Aurum, the other by *Aur. met.* and *China*, the particulars of which are herewith transcribed in his own quaint style :—

" Two cases only occurred in my experience, one was in company with gonorrhœa. The patient went hunting in damp cold weather while suffering from the clap, and returned with violent pains in both testicles. In the succeeding night the disease increased, and both testicles were swollen hard, not bearing the least touch ; the scrotum was red and tense ; some fever set in, which lasted till the evening of the next day. The gonorrhœa had ceased almost entirely.

" Two doses of *Clematis*, 12th dilution, three globules repeated at intervals of three days, cured the disease, whereupon the clap returned. The swelling of the other testicle, which continued longer, was cured by *Aurum metallicum* iv∞.

" The second case was a relapse of a previously endured inflammation of the testicle, allopathically treated, which yielded to *Aur. met.* iv∞ and *China* iv∞."

9. OPHTHALMIA.—Among the varied complications which attend an attack of gonorrhœa, there are none which inflict so much torture on the patient, or leave in its train so destructive and ghastly a group of phenomena as that dangerous metastatic form termed Gonorrhœal Ophthalmia, often caused by contact of purulent matter from the urethra, which consists of a violent inflammation of the mucous membrane of the eyeball and lids, attended with profuse discharge of matter closely resembling in all its properties that

which issues from the inflamed urethra in clap, and having some connection with the latter complaint.

In an acute and fully developed case we can generally trace three distinct stages. The first sets in with a violent burning and itching at the margin of the *lids* and *canthi*, accompanied by a profuse flow of acrid tears, and considerable *photophobia;* the conjunctiva is uniformly reddened, and the lids, particularly the upper ones, are considerably swollen, with a highly vascular engorgement of that portion of the membrane which extends from the lids to the eyeball ; there is acceleration of the pulse, fever, dulness of the head, a coated tongue, and constant thirst.

In a few days the second stage commences with considerable swelling of the conjunctiva, producing that condition termed *chemosis*. At first there is a whitish-yellow mucus, which speedily increases in quantity, and after awhile it assumes a greenish tint ; the pain now becomes *extremely acute*, and extends to the surrounding parts of the head and face. If this condition is not quickly arrested by proper means, it soon terminates in the third stage, and with it ulceration, sloughing, or opacity of the cornea, prolapsus of the iris, adhesions of the iris and cornea, followed frequently by suppuration, total disorganization and collapse of the whole globe. All the symptoms of vascular congestion are likewise present in an intense degree, attended with the most agonizing pain and tension, hemicrania, intolerance of light, and severe constitutional disturbance. Some idea of the severity of this inflammation may be conceived when it is stated that of fourteen cases related by that eminent surgeon, the late Mr. Lawrence, vision was entirely destroyed in *nine*, and in three of the remaining five there was partial opacity of the cornea, and anterior adhesions of the iris.

TREATMENT.—This is a complicated form which calls for the most prompt and energetic handling, both locally as well as constitutionally, and in addition to the faithful *Aconite, Belladonna, Merc. sol.*, and *Corrosivus* as internal remedies, recourse should be had to the topical application of a solution of *Alum, Sulphate of Zinc, Bichloride of Mercury*, or the *Nitrate of Silver*, whilst the eye itself and inner surface of the lids should be cleansed *six* or *seven* times a day with a tepid solution of *Carbolic Acid* or *Condy's* fluid. Ten cases of this type have come under my notice ; one was treated *allopathically*, some years since, by means of leeches, blisters, purgatives, scarifications, and the topical application of *Nitrate of Silver* according to the formula of Guthrie. In spite, however, of such heroic treatment, ulceration of the cornea set in, followed by a deep layer of opacity and loss of vision. The remaining cases were treated *homœopathically*, and with far more satisfactory results. They were seen in the first stages. *Aconite*, first decimal, was administered every two hours, as the "deep intense pain, redness of the lids and conjunctiva, swelling, pulsation, and profuse lachrymation, indicated the action of that medicine." These symptoms were considerably toned down, but did not prevent the disease from assuming a *muco-purulent* form, which was successfully combated in each case by *Merc. cor.*, second decimal, in alternation with *Aconite*, the frequent washing of the eye and inner surface of the lids with a solution of *Carbolic Acid* and water by means of a soft sponge and a syringe, followed each time by the injection of a solution of *Nitrate of Silver* of the following proportions :—Arg. nit. gr. iv., distilled water ℨiij.

In the chronic stage *Sulphur* is sufficient to complete the cure, which was accomplished in one case in fourteen days ; in the other cases, at the expiration of three weeks.

10. RHEUMATISM.—Before bringing this section of my labours to a close, I would briefly refer to another complication, which I think fairly completes that circle of complications which more or less attend an attack of Gonorrhœa, namely, *Gonorrhœal Rheumatism.*

This proves a very painful and obstinate symptom, and supervenes upon that complaint in from ten to thirty days from the first appearance of the urethral discharge, which at this stage becomes considerably diminished, and sometimes entirely stopped.

It generally attacks young persons of delicate, strumous constitutions, and others who have necessarily exposed themselves to cold, wet, or sudden changes of temperature.

The leading SYMPTOMS are—a severe aching or acute burning in one or more joints, generally the knees and ankles, followed by a rapid effusion within the capsules and bursæ, which become greatly distended. There is no perceptible redness or inflammation on the external surface, a peculiarity worth noting, but the pain is considerably aggravated by motion, and by the warmth of the bed. The affected limb is usually kept in a semi-flexed position, while

stretching or bending it tends to increase the sufferings of the patient.

The tongue is usually loaded with a brownish
mucus ; there is more or less fever and thirst ; the
pulse is quick, and sometimes rises to 120 strokes in
the minute ; the bowels are costive ; the perspiration
profuse and offensive ; the urine is scanty and highly
charged with lithates. These symptoms under favourable circumstances may subside in the course of two or
three weeks, but they too often terminate in a chronic
state, which may continue to torment the patient for
some months. This occurred to me some years ago
while in practice at Dover. The patient, a youth of nineteen, and of a highly strumous diathesis, was treated
by an allopathic practitioner with large doses of
Copaiva, which seriously disarranged the whole
system. In that condition he went out boating, caught
cold, which checked the urethral discharge, and terminated in a severe attack of rheumatism. He was
treated by the same official for another six weeks, but
with no relief to any of the symptoms. I was then requested to see him, and prescribed an occasional dose
of *Aconite* at bedtime, with *Puls.* and *Sulphur* in alternation : a series of lamp baths, and packings, which was
soon followed by a marked improvement. He was
then sent out in one of his father's ships to China,
and was fairly rid of his rheumatic companion ere
he sighted the shores of the Celestial Empire.

Aconite and *Pulsatilla* have done good service in
three cases of the acute form of rheumatism of
this type which have occurred in my own practice ; the former quickly subdued the febrile and

inflammatory symptoms ; the latter, completely re-establishing the urethral discharge. Two were convalescent in fourteen days, the third within twenty-eight days. In the chronic form I would suggest the selection of such remedies as *Merc. sol., Merc. vivus, Pulsatilla, Sarsaparilla, Thuja,* and *Sulph. ;* the frequent use of the lamp, or Turkish bath ; an occasional pack ; sea air ; a resort to the thermal springs of Bath, or Wiesbaden ; and finally, a long sea voyage.

GONORRHŒA IN WOMEN.

Gonorrhœa is both of less frequency, and greater difficulty of detection in women than in men. The reasons for this include the following ; viz., the less sensitiveness of the mucous membrane lining the genital organs of the female, as compared with that of the urethra in the male ; its being constantly bathed in its own natural secretions ; the protected position of the urethra ; and the absence in men of the menstrual flux and leucorrhœal discharge, which we have already found to be so fruitful a cause of the disease in the opposite sex.

The disease presents itself for consideration, however, under four different phases :—

1. When it attacks the vulva, as gonorrhœal VULVITIS.

2. When it attacks the mucous membrane of the urethra, as URETHRITIS.

3. When it attacks the vagina, which is the most usual and common form, as VAGINITIS.

4. When the interior of the uterus becomes involved,

F

as UTERITIS. As the symptoms and treatment, however, differ, it would be well to describe them separately, premising, however, that they may be, and usually are, more or less combined in each case.

1. GONORRHŒAL VULVITIS is a specific inflammation of the mucous membrane of the external organs of generation, and corresponds to balanitis in the male. The early symptoms are—heat of the .part and a troublesome pruritus, whilst on examination the mucous membrane will be seen to be of a deeper colour than natural, slightly swollen, and moist. This condition soon becomes aggravated, and there is severe aching pain, which is increased by motion or by touch, with superficial excoriations, scalding on urinating, bearing-down pains, and a feeling of weight in the external genitals. The discharge from it, being simply albuminous at first, assumes after a time a purulent character, and is most irritating and offensive. It is the most painful variety of gonorrhœa, and perhaps the most distressing complication is, a form of "Nymphomania," which is occasionally present. Small abscesses also are apt to form in the vicinity of the vulvo-vaginal glands.

2. GONORRHŒAL URETHRITIS.—The urethral form of gonorrhœa is rarely met with alone in the female; but it usually co-exists with that of the vulva or vagina. It is indicated by a burning pain along the urethra, which is greatly intensified on micturating. There is but little discharge, but the lips of the meatus are swollen and painful, and the introduction of a catheter causes the most excruciating agony. The finger, when introduced *per vaginam,* detects a

thickening of the canal ; and if pressure be made against the pubic arch, it will feel as firm as a piece of whipcord. Fortunately, this variety is not liable, as in the male, to degenerate into a gleet ; but abscesses, however, occasionally form in the vagina and perinæum, and often the glands in the groin suppurate as well.

3. GONORRHŒAL VAGINITIS.—The vagina is more frequently the seat of gonorrhœa than any other part of the mucous tract. When seen at an early period the membrane looks red, is hot, and devoid of moisture. Itching, smarting pains, with frequent desire to pass water, and dull aching are complained of in the hypogastric region. The vagina feels hot and puffy, and soon secretes a large quantity of offensive purulent or muco-purulent matter, of a yellow, or milky, or greenish ichorous character. In the course of a few days the discharge decreases in quantity, the disease now becomes chronic, and is extremely difficult of eradication. It will usually be found that the anterior half of the vagina, immediately under the arch of the pubis, is the part affected, and presents an aphthous appearance when examined with the aid of the speculum. As there is in the chronic stage generally some degree of vulvitis, we often see a warty and even condylomatous condition of the labia majora as well.

4. GONORRHŒAL UTERITIS.—Gonorrhœa but seldom attacks the internal surface of the uterus, except as an extension from the vagina. When it is present the disease assumes a most serious aspect. The ovaries are apt to become implicated, the general

health undermined, and the reproductive processes interfered with. The uterus becomes congested, the os excoriated, and usually we have a constant oozing from it of a highly offensive, gluey, yellowish-white matter. The bladder and rectum also sympathize, and both defæcation and urination are painful.

This form of the disease is difficult to diagnose and to cure, and, we have little doubt, is for the most part left behind as leucorrhœa ; either from want of cleanliness or care in the patient, or through inappropriate medication by the practitioner.

DIAGNOSIS.—It is admitted by all experienced observers to be all but impossible to differentiate in some cases between gonorrhœa and leucorrhœa,. but fortunately homœopathy furnishes us with such weapons wherewith to attack the disease, that it is not of much importance. The moral symptoms, however, of the patient will be the best guide to a correct diagnosis.

TREATMENT.—This will vary, more or less, according to the stage and seat of the malady.

1. VULVITIS will require a similar treatment to balanitis in the male. Great cleanliness, warm emollient fomentations, and frequently repeated doses of *Mercurius* and *Aconite* in the acute stage ; whilst the chronic form will be best cured by *Alum* or *Tannic acid* lotions, *Thuja*, and *Sulphur*.

2. VAGINITIS.—If we are fortunately called in at the commencement of the attack, we give *Bell.* and *Merc.* or *Puls.* in alternation every three hours, order the patient to sit over hot marsh-mallow fomentations every six hours, and take a hot sitz bath every night at bedtime. When the acute symptoms have

been subdued, or have passed away before the case presents itself for treatment, we find *Kreasote* or *Sepia*, especially the latter, afford the most efficient aid. Slightly astringent injections, as *Alum* gr. ij. to water ʒj., or alterative ones, as *Tr. hydrastis* ʒss. to water ʒviij., will sometimes be found of great benefit.

3. URETHRITIS.—Here the treatment will be essentially the same as in gonorrhœa in the male, though of course injections will help but little. *Aconite* and *Cantharides*, followed by *Cannabis sativa* and *Sulphur*, according to presenting symptoms, will soon eradicate this form of the complaint.

4. UTERITIS.—This is the most difficult form to treat, and probably is but seldom cured, unless a very correct diagnosis is established.

The acute symptoms must be met by *Aconite* and *Canth.* or *Nitric acid ;* and *Sepia* or *Platina* may be pretty reliably expected to cure the chronic form.

Here, as in vaginitis also, we require injections ; they should be introduced into the cavity of the uterus by means of a proper instrument ; and I know of none which can compete with either *Tannic acid,* or the *Hydrastic canadensis.*

Three cases of gonorrhœal uteritis have come under my notice within the last six years. The last case was that of a London *Demi-monde* who consulted me at Cambridge about three years ago. She was in the habit of paying periodical visits to that classic seat of learning, and kept her "TERMS" with as much regularity as the most studious and industrious undergraduate that struts along under the canopy of those grand old avenues which adorn the equally classic grounds of King's and Trinity. She frankly and unreservedly confessed to me the nature of her "professional calling;" that she was much perplexed to know what to do; and that although she indulged in frequent ablutions, and the use of a syringe three or four times a day, although she had consulted some of the leading syphilographers in London for eighteen months, and had visited two of its Lock Hospitals; yet, in spite of all this, every man who approached this "Sirenic Goddess"—and they were many—left her chamber inoculated with the seed of gonorrhœa. But the most astounding part of her narrative was, that out of the numerous medical men she had consulted, not one even suggested the womb as being the source from whence the foul virus might have emanated. A careful and steady dilatation of the mouth of the womb, by means of sponge and sea weed tents, enabled me at the expiration of four days to obtain an excellent view of the interior of the organ, where the cause of all the mischief was soon discovered. A solution of *Tannic acid*, with a slight dash of *Condy's fluid*, was injected night and morning, and at the expiration of seven days all discharge had disappeared. A similar mode of treatment was adopted in the other cases. One, more obstinate than the other, and where I suspected a syphilitic taint as well, yielded to the combined action of the lotion and *Mercurius vivus* 3x in the course of one month.

PART II.

CHANCROID AND ITS COMPLICATIONS.

LET us now briefly consider the second subdivision of this truly Protean disease.

SYNONYMOUSLY—the *common, simple, soft, non-infecting, non-indurated,* or *superficial chancre,* with raised edges.

The *chancroid* of Bassereux, the *false* or *local syphilis* of Ricord, Lancereux, and others.

Its chief characteristics are—

1. Its period of INCUBATION, which seldom extends beyond three or four days, but generally appears within twenty-four hours of an impure coition.

2. Its supposed localization.

3. Its marked power of multiplying itself by successive inoculations ; consequently it seldom appears alone, but is attended by two, three, or more sores of a like kind.

4. Its frequent termination in suppurative buboes.

Lastly. Its tendency to produce a very painful and destructive group of complications of a local character.

In form this ulcer is somewhat oval, flat, superficial, with raised and well-marked edges ; it has a tendency to spread and burrow beneath the sound skin ; it secretes a thin, profuse *ichorous* fluid or yellowish pus ; and often throws out indolent fungous granulations.

In the male it is found both on the external and
.internal surface of the prepuce ; sometimes on the
" corona glandis ; sometimes garnishing the outer
margin of the prepuce in the form of a wreath ; and
sometimes it invades one side of the frænum, which
is soon destroyed, if not quickly checked by proper
treatment."

In the female we generally find it on the *labia
majora et minora*.   It is a form of the venereal disease
which appears much more frequently than its allied
representative of the fourteenth century.   Amongst
10,000 chancres recorded by Puche, there were found
of—

> Soft or chancroid sores   ...   8,045
> Indurated, or Hunterian sores, 1,955

And amongst 341 chancres observed and recorded by
Fournier there were found of—

> Indurated sores   126
> Soft or chancroid sores   ...   215

The power of this form of sore for self-inoculation
is very remarkable, as it is no uncommon thing for
some patients to have as many as *three, four, five, six,*
and even *fifteen* sores at the same time.   Lindmann,
according to that eminent syphilographer Ricord,
effected on his own person more than 2,200 primary
inoculations.

The course of a simple chancre is continuous and
progressive, and after a certain time, which seldom
exceeds a month, the ulcer ceases to spread.   Its floor
then becomes clean, its surface covered with red or pink
granulations, which secrete a healthy yellow pus.
·The redness and swelling disappear ; in short, the

contagious virus loses its specific character, and the ulcer becomes transformed into a simple sore ; whilst cicatrices form from the circumference towards the centre. Such, then, is a brief outline of an ordinary case of "a soft chancre ; " but in many cases it exhibits a strong tendency to strike out, invade and destroy neighbouring tissues, and establishes as " outposts " a very painful and destructive group of—

COMPLICATIONS—such as that virulent suppurating BUBO in the inguinal region, whose ravages at times are so frightful as to lay bare *muscles, nerves, vessels, tendons*, and even the *bones ;* undermining to its very foundation the strongest constitution, and secreting a virulent pus, of a similar character to that of the chancre which caused it.

It will sometimes create a very painful and dangerous form of PHIMOSIS and PARAPHIMOSIS, rendered still more painful and complicated by the series of ulcers and excoriations which are frequently found studding the glans and prepuce. It will sometimes assume a creeping form, the SERPIGINOUS SORE of some writers. At other times it will ultimate into a still more virulent form, the PHAGEDÆNIC SORE, which, as its name implies (φαγω, to eat), is an angry, corroding ulcer, highly painful, rapid and destructive in its progress ; irregular in form, the edges ragged and undermined ; the surface yellow, and dotted with red specks. It sometimes eats deeply into the substance of the penis ; at other times it undermines the skin ; but in general it spreads superficially and rapidly, carrying, " like a prairie fire," destruction and death in its course, until the whole

or the greater portion of the genital tissues are totally
disorganized, and sometimes irremediably destroyed.

It is destitute of any marked degree of surrounding
hardness; but the skin encircling the sore looks
puffy, swollen, and of a vivid red colour, whilst the
ulcer itself bleeds freely, showing an inflammatory
and depraved condition of arterial action.

GANGRENE is another type which this terrible and
destructive ulcer sometimes assumes, and frequently
exhibits that characteristic form within the first few
days of the existence of the ulcer. It generally presents itself as a red circle, more or less bright in
colour; the surface is tumefied and covered with
brownish points, and secretes a dirty or rusty-coloured
pus ; the circle becomes deeper and deeper, the parts
included in it assume a grey, brown, or sometimes
a blackish tint, which finally becomes detached.
The slough so formed will sometimes attack a portion
of the prepuce only, at other times it will invade a large
portion, or even the whole of the *glans,* leaving considerable destruction of the parts behind it.

DIPHTHERITIC, and a "thrush-like secretion is
sometimes found deposited on this kind of sore, the
floor of which assumes a yellowish tint, and mixed with
bloody striæ ; the edges are of a violet colour, and the
surrounding tissues considerably swollen. The patient
complains of considerable pain, the pulse is quick,
he loses his appetite, and has generally much fever.
The presence of this pultaceous deposit, has a tendency
to blunt the sensibility of the chancre, as the latter
becomes insensible to external agents, and sometimes
even to the action of cauterization.

This phagedænic and gangrenous chancre may appear in a *primary* form, or a *secondary* form. The primary is usually met with in weakened, vitiated, or scrofulous constitutions; the secondary type as a consequence of neglecting a primary sore, by abandoning one's self to filth, intemperance, an irregular and depraved diet, the use and abuse of mercury, and having connection with women whilst in such a diseased condition of body and depraved condition of health. A case of this kind came under my notice in 1867, which I consider worth recording as an instance of the depravity of human nature, and as an illustration of the transfer of a simple sore, to a foul, gangrenous, and destructive one.

The patient, a man of thirty-eight to forty years old, had been leading a very debauched life for some days, by luxuriating in some of the London hells by night, and sleeping in some of the lowest brothels by day. On the fourth or fifth day of such a career, he observed a sore on the penis, which he deemed unworthy of notice, and, reckless of consequences, continued to pursue the same course. On the ninth day, "but not before he had disseminated the foul poison far and wide," his reckless mission was brought to a close, by the total transmission of a simple chancre into a black gangrenous mass. He then sought the counsel of a chemist, who, ignorant of the character of the sore, plied him freely with blue pill and black wash; this only added fuel to the fire, which blazed away at such a terrific pace as to well-nigh destroy the whole appendage. On the twelfth day, at 9 p.m., I was summoned to the bed-

side of that man, who, in the agonies of pain and a
stricken conscience, was appealing lustily to high
heaven for forgiveness.   Nearly the whole of his penis
was one blackened fœtid mass, from whence emanated a stench of the foulest description, which
permeated the whole room.   This was a case which
demanded prompt attention, and energetic treatment ;
there could be no parleying with such an enemy, or
coaxing with the 30th dilution of any medicine.
Like uterine hæmorrhage, or a wounded vessel, it
demanded immediate and effectual means to save life.
One application of strong *Nitric acid* sufficed to
check the onward march of the enemy; the member
was afterwards wrapped in a warm bread and water
poultice, and in twelve hours the whole of the charred
mass dropped off, bringing to view a reddened exca-
vated surface ; this was dressed with a weak solution
of *Nitric acid*, which was also administered internally,
being the only medicine prescribed.   In three weeks
this patient was convalescent, save a very ugly de-
formity in the contour of his penis.

   There is another form of the phagedænic and
gangrenous chancre which is still more severe and
destructive than the one we have just considered, but
not often encountered west of Temple Bar ; namely,
the sloughing ulcer—better known at some of the
London hospitals, particularly those situated in the
Borough and East End, as "the Swan Alley sore."
The late Mr. Travers has described this form of
chancre with great accuracy, and states that the
genuine type is usually seen in very young girls
who reside in a place called Swan Alley, situate

near St. Katharine's Docks, who have intercourse with sailors, Lascars, Negroes, and other dirty foreign seamen, as many times in the day as there are hours. It usually shows itself in the cleft of the nates, in the groin, or on one of the labia towards the perinæum, and as it enlarges, the surrounding skin puts on a crimson colour ; the surface of the sore is covered with a deep ash-coloured slough,—in fact, a kind of diphtheritic deposit. This form of sore extends with alarming rapidity, and produces great constitutional disturbance and intense pain ; the appetite is lost, and extreme prostration of strength attends the disease throughout the greater part of its course. We further learn from the same able authority that most of the young girls brought from that locality have but little wholesome food, being generally kept by Jews and Jewesses, who ply them with plenty of gin and other ardent spirits, though with but little proper nourishment. In this manner their constitutions very soon get into a depraved condition, and extremely disadvantageous for the favourable progress of any disease ; consequently it is not to be wondered that their impaired, imperfectly developed frames, their wretched course of life, their uncleanliness, their constant indulgence in ardent spirits of the worst kind, and the deprivation of pure air and wholesome food should promote phagedænic ulceration, and give it a more than ordinary severe character.

Two cases of this form came under my notice four years ago, the respective ages of the patients being sixteen and nineteen. In the younger there were two large ragged ulcers, one on each cleft of the nates, in the other nearly the whole of the left labia majora was destroyed, each being covered by a deep ash-coloured slough, and each bled profusely.

These cases were treated with *Nitric acid* both internally and externally, and *Aconite* at bedtime ; a cold sitz bath night and morning, a generous diet, with half a pint of good sound claret daily ; and at the expiration of four weeks a very satisfactory cure in each case was effected.

It may here be observed that these phagedænic ulcers and sloughing sores may occur as a *complication* of any kind of ulcers, whether they be of the Hunterian or the chancroid type ; and that such unfavourable changes often depend on constitutional, climacteric, dietetic, hygienic, and therapeutic causes ; such as a scrofulous or broken-down constitution ; ill-ventilated and badly drained courts and alleys, such as we find in the purlieus of St. Giles, the rookery at Westminster, and the habitat of the London Arab in the far east ; intemperance ; an irregular and depraved mode of living ; and particularly the reckless administration of mercurial preparations, " which I have witnessed in many cases to produce the most frightful and destructive forms of phagedæna," may likewise be set down as causes.

It is also, I think, a well-established fact that a woman may communicate to man, under peculiar circumstances, a phagedænic sore of a very aggravated form, although she may at the time have but a trivial complaint herself.. This was well exemplified in the case of the celebrated Lisbon opera dancer, which has now become an historic fact. The late Mr. Samuel

Cooper, of University College Hospital, was wont to relate in his own happy style, the circumstances connected with that captivating woman, whose charms attracted so many officers of the British army into her embraces during the Peninsular war, while great numbers of them received as a reward for their adoration of that irresistible goddess the present of something more than a trifling clap. Indeed, such was the CORROSIVE and DESTRUCTIVE nature of that phagedænic sore that it received the name of the BLACK LION. And yet that woman continued to dance every night for months together as if she were perfectly healthy; whilst her gallant adorers were suffering the torments of the damned inflicted upon them through the power of so fascinating a goddess, whose poison, like that of the viper, hurt not herself.

In the treatment of A CHANCROID SORE and its complications it is seldom I have had occasion to travel beyond the range of *Acid nit.*, *Arsenicum*, *Causticum*, and the *Potassio-tartrate of iron ;* strict cleanliness; the local application of a solution of the former and latter, and sometimes *Carbolic acid* or *Condy's fluid*, with a judiciously selected diet.

Acid. nit. I hold to be as formidable an opponent to the so-called soft sore, as the *Merc. sol.* is to the hard "Hunterian" chancre. Its symptomatical effects on the body in health prove this in a marked degree ; thus it causes—

Frequent itching of the glans.

Red spots on the glans, which become **covered with scabs.**

Deep ulcers on the glans, with elevated, lead-coloured, sensitive edges.

Inflammation and swelling of the prepuce, with a burning pain.

Swelling of the prepuce—phymosis.

Chancre-like sores, with flat edges, studding the internal surface and border of the prepuce, attended with lancinating pains.

Small itching vesicles on the prepuce.

In the female it causes irritation, and inflammation of the labia majora et minora, with ulcers in the vagina, covered with yellow pus, and attended with itching, burning pains. From these provings we infer that *Acid nit.* stands foremost as a curative agent in that form of "pseudo-syphilis" sometimes found at the orifice of the urethra; the edge and inner surface of the prepuce, at the root of the corona glandis, and close to the frænum, presenting a somewhat oval form; the edges well marked, flat, and painless; the surface perceptibly raised above the margin; clean, flesh-coloured, and fungus-like; secreting a thin, fœtid, ichorous, sanguineous pus, which does not adhere to the sore, is easily wiped away, and moreover has no perceptible hardness at its base, and with no distinguishing difference between it and the surrounding surface.

In ordinary cases of this type, I prescribe the acid in the second or third decimal dilution, repeated three or four times a day; conjoined with strict cleanliness, the application of a solution of *Calendula, Carbolic acid,* or *Nitric acid* to the ulcers, and a good plain diet. Such cases generally get well within from

fourteen to eighteen days. Attomyr, who had considerable experience in venereal diseases, invariably prescribed this medicine with the same satisfactory results.
In the common superficial ulcer, says that author, *Acid.
nit.* is the principal remedy when it exists without any
complications : the acid acts very soon, and at farthest
in twenty days the disease is cured. Gollmann states,
" Among the remedies to be employed for the cure of
chancre I mention particularly *Acidum nitricum,*
the specific effect of which has scarcely ever disappointed me." Allopathic authorities, from John
Hunter to the present day, recommend excision and
cauterization, as a means of curing this form of
chancre. " The most simple method of treating a
chancre," says Hunter, " consists in destroying or
extirpating it." " To reduce a *specific* ulcer to the condition of a *simple* ulcer," says Ricord, " appears to be
the proper object of the treatment ; and cauterization,
if sufficiently deep, fulfils this purpose." It is performed
by various substances, such as the *Carbo-sulphuric*
paste of RICORD ; the *Chloride of Zinc* paste of DIDAY ;
the actual cautery at a white heat of ROLLET ; or the
Potassa fusa, Potassa cum Calce, or strong *Nitric
acid,* as recommended by PARKER.

I am, however, firmly of opinion, which is borne out
by more than an ordinary amount of experience, that
there exists no necessity whatever for the use of such
severe and brutal measures in the ordinary form of
soft chancres ; and I further attest that some of the
most severe and complicated çases which have come
under my immediate notice were in a great measure
çaused by such vicious meddlings—quaintly, but too

G

truly described by Attomyr as *plasterings, corrodings, incising, re-corroding,* and *re-incising,* methods pursued in old physic.

It should be borne in mind that a soft chancre has a strong tendency to assume an irritable form ; to re-inoculate itself *ad libitum ;* to creep along or spread abroad, and transfer a portion of its virus to the inguinal glands, where it establishes the most HIDEOUS and DESTRUCTIVE forms of suppurative buboes ; it is, moreover, allied with a peculiar and *specific* form of inflammation, which may assume the adhesive, the *suppurative, ulcerative,* or *gangrenous* form; in fact it sets up an inflammation " sui generis," and of a peculiarly irritable nature. To treat such a sore by such means as are here recommended, would only be adding fuel to the fire. Twenty-three cases of this type of sore which have come under my notice within the last sixteen months, yielded kindly enough to *Nitric acid* and *Carbolic acid* dressing, an occasional poultice when inflammation ran high, and *Aconite* at bedtime ; which invariably had a very soothing and tranquillizing effect on the nervous system.

Causticum is clearly indicated when a series of sores appear under the prepuce, secreting an acrid, corrosive pus of a watery or greenish colour, with a disposition to fungous formations, occurring in persons of a gouty disposition, or those subject to cutaneous eruptions. I generally prescribe this medicine in the second and third decimal dilutions.

Arsenicum steps in as an admirable remedy when the sore assumes the gangrenous form, with bloody edges, secreting a corrosive, watery, fœtid discharge,

occurring in weak, scrofulous, or broken-down constitutions : in such cases the potency should not
exceed the second or third decimal, in which dose
it acts as a powerful tonic, irrespective of its homœopathicity to the condition of the ulcer. Fowler's
solution also offers a ready and useful form for the
administration of this drug.

Potassio-tartrate of iron.—I have seen very satisfactory results follow the administration of this drug
in a large number of cases which came under my notice
while watching for some time the treatment of venereal
diseases at one of the London Lock Hospitals. It
is one of Ricord's favourite remedies, who styles it
the "born enemy" of the soft chancre, and prescribes
it as follows :—

Distilled water . . . 250 parts,
Potassio-tartrate of iron . 30 „

Mix. Three tablespoonfuls to be taken daily. The
sore to be dressed three times a day with lint dipped
in this solution.

PART III.

TRUE SYPHILIS.

IN the former sections of this monograph it has been endeavoured to set forth, in as succinct a form as compatible with space, in what the historical evidences concerning SYPHILITIC and SYPHILOIDAL diseases consist. These, with the help of authorities of un-impeachable veracity, have enabled us to trace its course from the remotest landmarks of civilization to the present time ; and we have seen step by step its peculiar characteristics stamped with indelible màrks upon the historic page of every people possessing records worthy of credence. We have referred to its analogous diseases—to its contagious origin ; and we have disposed of two of its main subdivisions, namely, the so-called local *gonorrhœa* and its painful complica-tions ; the *chancroid* with its suppurating *buboes*, its *phagedœnic* and *gangrenous* complications ; but a very important section of our task still remains to be considered, constituting the third subdivision of my programme, namely, the *Syphilis* of Fracastorius, 1514 ; the *Leues Venerea* of Fernel, 1530 ; the *Pestilential Scorra* of Joseph Grundpeck, 1496 ; the *Morbus Gallico* of Nicolus Leonicenus, 1496 ; the *De Dolore in Puden-dagra* of Gaspar Torella, 1500 ; the *Grose Verole* of the French ; the *indurated sore* of the great John Hunter ; the *indurated, non-suppurating, syphilitic, infecting chancre* of Lancereux; in a word, the "Hunterian chancre," with its constitutional ravages of modern Europe, and the civilized world.

Whilst dwelling on the records of the past, we can plainly see that syphilis proper is constantly indicated, but the indications remain symptomatic, and only symptomatic. No general definition has as yet been promulgated sufficiently concise and comprehensive to meet the requirements of the present age. Into the intimate nature of syphilis, *in essentia*, we have not yet been able to penetrate, surrounded as it is by such a halo of mystery. It nevertheless becomes an important question to inquire in how far others have already defined syphilis, and by their definitions endeavour to attain some certainty to guide us in the further prosecution of the search. We shall therefore proceed to quote several definitions from authorities to which all schools of medicine are agreed to pay respectful deference. Of these we would first refer to the ancients.

In 1493, Joseph Grundpeck defined it as a *plague* sent down from the citadel of the immortal gods upon the French; a most horrid and terrible prodigy—a disease repugnant to nature, and formerly *unseen*, *unknown*, and quite *unheard of*. In the same year Alexander Benedict, of Verona, attributed it to a pestiferous aspect of the stars, and that it first burst in upon them from the west.

In 1530, John Fernel—surnamed the modern Galen—defined it as a disease in which the whole of the body is morbific, being contagious, presenting tubercles, spots, ·ulcers, sores, and pains, produced in succession, either from the act of a single concubinage or from other impure contact.

John Hunter was of opinion that the effects produced by the syphilitic poison arose from its peculiar or specific irritation, joined with the aptness of the living principle to be irritated by such a cause, and the parts so irritated acting accordingly. Hence he considered that the virus irritated the living parts in a manner peculiar to itself, and produced an inflammation peculiar to that irritation, from which a matter is produced peculiar to the inflammation.

In Nysten's dictionary there is the following definition :—" Syphilis is a specific malady, not spontaneous, transmitted by contact and heritage, characterized at its different periods by certain accidents, the evolution of which is subordinated to the action of the syphilitic virus, the course of which is usually determined."

Wallace defines syphilis as a specific morbid poison, which when applied to the human body has the power of propagating or multiplying itself, and capable of acting both locally and constitutionally.

Samuel Cooper defines it as certain morbid changes produced in various textures of the human body by the action of a specific morbid poison.

Attomyr denominates as syphilitic every disorder presented by *Venus Pandamos* to her votaries, and first exhibited on the organs of reproduction.

Franklin defines it as a specific disease transmitted by means of its own peculiar virus, coming in contact with an abraded surface, by inoculation through the medium of the secretions, or by hereditary descent.

Ricord only gives a general definition, and states

that syphilis is a contagious disease engendered by a virus commencing by a peculiar affection — the CHANCRE; syphilis springs from a chancre, and recognises no other origin.

Lancereux defines syphilis as a specific disease, transmissible by *contact* or by *inheritance;* characterized by a slow periodical progressive development, and especially by changes in the cellular tissue, without direct tendency to suppuration, being acquired or hereditary,—the former by contagion or inoculation, the latter traceable to father or mother already infected.

Finally, Astruc, in his remarkable work on the "History and Pathology of Syphilis" (1754), in endeavouring to define syphilis—or, as he called it, "the confirmed pox"—says: "The nature of this disease is of so wide an extent, and it comprehends such an infinite number of different symptoms, that it rather appears to be a world of diseases than one ; therefore it were vain to attempt a definition of a disease that cannot be comprehended within the narrow limits of a definition ; and it is much better to place in one view the nature, form and disposition of this disease, and the series and connection of the effects which it produces, by an accurate description and enumeration of its more remarkable symptoms."

With such a definition we must be content; and with the closing remarks of that eminent physician I quite agree ; let us therefore proceed to examine briefly the peculiar characteristics of this terrible form of the *venereal* disease, with a description and enumeration of its more remarkable phenomena.

SYPHILIS is essentially a constitutional disease,

and, according to Ricord, is divisible into three
periods :—

1. PRIMARY LESION, a chancre, the result of contagion.

2. SECONDARY LESIONS, or constitutional poisoning,
resulting from that infection.

3. TERTIARY LESIONS, which rarely show themselves before the end of the sixth month.   To these I
would add—

4. QUATERNARY LESIONS, constituting the invasion
of the various viscera.

Lancereux, however, not quite satisfied with the
above arrangement, proposes the following classification, as more clearly showing certain analogies of
evolution between that disease and some of those
termed EPIDEMIC and VIRULENT, namely :—

A. The period of incubation.

B. The period of local eruption, a *chancre*, or *primary
lesion.*

C. The period of general eruption, otherwise
secondary symptoms.

D. The period of gummy products, otherwise
tertiary and *quaternary affections.*

This arrangement is a decided improvement on the
former, as we have here, well-defined prominent
landmarks separating each of these periods.

In the first, there is complete absence of any local
manifestations.   In the second, we have outward
manifestations in the form of a *pustule* at the supposed
spot where the contagious virus first entered—I say
" supposed," for no one has yet ever seen it.   In the
third, we have numerous superficial lesions; and in

the fourth, we have more deep-seated lesions, followed by extensive disorganizations and cicatrices.

Let us therefore proceed according to Lancereux's classification.

By INCUBATION, it should be understood as embracing the interval of time which elapses between the moment of the absorption of the syphilitic virus and that of the appearance of the first local manifestation—the chancre.

The period of *incubation* in syphilis, we find, bears a singular analogy to the general symptomatology of other *febrile, epidemic,* and *contagious* disorders. We quote the following periods as examples.

In yellow fever there is a period of incubation varying from ... ... 3 to 10 days.

In small-pox	12 to 16 „
„ scarlet fever	4 to 6 „
„ measles	6 to 16 „
„ typhus	2 to 12 „
„ typhoid	10 to 18 „
„ chicken-pox	2 to 3 „
„ ague	10 to 14 „
„ diphtheria	2 to 6 „
„ cow-pox	2 to 6 „
„ erysipelas	3 to 7 „
„ hooping cough	6 to 10 „
„ the plague ... from a few hours to 3 weeks.
„ relapsing fever ... ... 3 to 6 days.
„ simple continued fever, generally only a few hours.
„ gonorrhœa ... ... 2 to 14 days.
„ dry papule ... ... 4 to 21 „
„ chancroid (soft chancre) ... 2 to 3 „

In TRUE SYPHILIS however, the period of incubation in the generality of cases ranges from SEVEN to TWENTY-ONE days from the occurrence of a coit ; and there are strong grounds for considering that the more or less rapid exhibition of the disease arises from a constitutional sympathy in the person receptive of contagion, thus regulating, as it were, the period of incubation. The disease being more actively absorbed, is more energetically protested against and repelled in cases of sanguine temperaments in proportion to the vital force of the recipient, and to the sympathy so constitutionally existing for diseases of a *contagious epidemic* nature. I would even urge that the germ of the disease is developed at the greatest period of excitement, when offspring is not thought of, but the mere gratification of *physical* and *animal* passion. The symptoms indicating the stage of incubation are sometimes well marked, and should be prominently remembered by those who run the risk of such infection, as they may be the means of sounding the *alarm bell* and seeking the early advice of their medical adviser. These may be set down as *dejection of spirits; pain in the head ; slow fever ; weight about the shoulders ; sleeplessness ; carelessness of employment ; indistinctness of vision ; general heaviness ; flying bone pains ; and loss of flesh.* Such, in fact, are the leading symptoms which have been described to me from time to time by those who have suffered from syphilitic affections. Prophylactic and private hygienic measures have been suggested by physicians from the historic period of ancient Rome and Greece to the present time. Celsus speaks of it at some length ;

Lanfranc (1290) and others advised washing the penis with vinegar and water; others lemon juice; some, solutions of *alum, tannic acid, lime water, alcohol,* and *corrosive sublimate;* and others, *fatty* and *oily* products. *Phenic acid,* more generally known as carbolic acid, may likewise be mentioned as an agent which, according to an eminent French authority, "is capable of neutralizing a certain number of animal poisons, and among these the poison of SYPHILIS;" but hitherto no satisfactory cases have been brought forward in confirmation of such a statement. The evidence we, however, possess of the remarkable prophylactic properties of *Belladonna* in *scarlet fever* and *small-pox,* "as attested by French authorities," of *Pulsatilla* in measles, of *vaccination* in small-pox, of *Quinine* in ague, and of *Cuprum* and *Veratrum* in Asiatic cholera; and the striking analogy that exists between the pathogenetic effects of MERCURY and SYPHILIS, lead me to infer that we may find in Hahnemann's celebrated preparation a most formidable opponent to the so-called incubated stage of that foul miasm. Here are its symptoms:—"Anguish, with lowness of spirits; pains in the head; low fever, with a feeble, slow, and trembling pulse; a general 'malaise;' pains about the shoulders, as if pressed down; sleeplessness, anxiety, and restlessness; excessive indifference to everything; dim-sightedness; general heaviness; all his bones ache, with general weakness, as if his limbs gave way." I would suggest that *two grains* of the *second decimal trituration* be taken *two* or *three* times a day for a period commensurate with the incubated stage of the syphilitic poison.

PERIOD OF LOCAL ERUPTION.—The primary lesion of true syphilis presents varied aspects, with which every student of medicine ought to be familiar, in order to be able to form a correct diagnosis. These we will set down in the following order :—

1.—The dry papule.

2.—The chancrous or chancriform erosion.

3.—The indurated or " Hunterian chancre."

1. DRY PAPULE.—This is the rarest of the different forms which syphilis assumes.

SYMPTOMS.—After an incubation of considerable duration, sometimes "weeks," there will appear at the supposed point of infection a papular patchy protuberance of a round or oval form, firm and elastic, of a dark or brownish red colour, and covered with *whitish* or *silvery* scales ; its base is *indurated*, it seldom or never suppurates, and gradually disappears by absorption, leaving behind it a slight violet-coloured or blackish depression. It is attended by the usual sympathetic buboes in the groins, and leaves in its wake constitutional symptoms, but of a mild form. Here is a case in point :—

J. L., æt. thirty-eight, a warehouseman in the City, consulted me November 12, 1870. Twelve months previously he observed what he termed a large pimple behind the corona glandis ; its base was hard, and felt like a *kernel*; its surface was covered with copper-coloured scales ; it never broke, but remained as such for some weeks, when it gradually diminished in size, and entirely disappeared, leaving behind a dark, violet-coloured depression. Some weeks afterwards he felt languid and dejected, his tongue felt larger than usual, his voice became husky, his tonsils enlarged, uvula elongated, and there appeared on the posterior palatine region, both tonsils, and sides of the tongue, superficial erosions. He was first treated allopathically, and took considerable quantities of mercury and *Potass. iod.* for some months before he consulted me, with no decided benefit. He was placed under *Aur. met.* and *Hep. sulph.*, and in three months all these symptoms disappeared.

2. CHANCROUS, OR CHANCRIFORM EROSIONS.— This, according to the statistics of Bassereau and Diday, is the most frequent form which primary syphilis presents; viz. 144 times in 170 cases. It coincides with the *patchy excoriation* of Carmichael ; the *superficial primary syphilis* of Wallace ; the *parch- ment-like chancre* of Ricord ; the *Venerola Vulgaris* of Evans ; the *condylomatous affection* of Renecker ; the *superficial erosion* of Langlebert ; the *chancrous erosion* of Bassereau ; and the *chancriform erosion* of Diday.

SYMPTOMS.—After an incubation of more or less duration there will appear on some part of the penis, most frequently behind the corona glandis, a copper- red spot, scarcely raised, papular and dry, which scales off, and becomes covered with a crust or thin scales, and is afterwards slightly ulcerated. In form it is round, or irregular ; the surface is flat, and level with the surrounding parts, the surface is rose- coloured, its base is indurated, more *superficially* than *deeply*, and secretes a scanty serous fluid. It is attended with the usual hard and indolent condition of the inguinal glands, and is followed by secondary symptoms, particularly in the form of mucous patches.

This form of chancre is sometimes covered with a *crust*, particularly when situated on the skin, or on any portion of the mucous membrane exposed to the air; it then assumes the character of *herpes, ecthyma*, or a squamous eruption. Attomyr termed it the *itch chancre*, and regarded it as a complication of *syphilis* and *itch*, which presumption was confirmed, not only by the form of the sore, but also by the violent itching of the same, and the favourable result which followed the administration of *Sulphur*. I am able to confirm the views propounded by that author, as I have met with several cases having the characteristic symptom of "itching," which quickly yielded to an occasional dose of *Sulphur*, given in alternation with its true specific, *Mercury*.

3. THE INDURATED, OR HUNTERIAN CHANCRE.— After a longer or shorter period of incubation, there will appear on some part of the penis a minute red spot, which is soon followed by an *elevation*, or *papule*, which gradually reaches the size of a *lentil*, or *pea ;* of a red or dirty yellow colour ; rounded and hard to the touch. This *papule* in the course of a short time becomes covered with greyish scales, which gradually become thicker, and end by forming in most cases a true crust, under which a *cup-shaped* ulcer of greater or less depth rapidly develops itself. It may also be described as having a sharp-edged circular form, as if cut with a punch : it has a glossy, iridescent surface, which is surrounded by a copper-coloured areola ; and a floor which is bathed with a *whitish-yellow, tough, gluey, corrosive, offensive* secretion, difficult of removal, and leaving stains on the linen like melted tallow—" lardaceous ;" its other characteristics are—

1. Its tendency to dip down instead of spreading.

2. The scanty and adhesive property of its secretion.

3. The peculiar hardness of its base, which feels when grasped between the thumb and forefinger like one half of a *split pea*, or a *cartilaginous cup* set in the flesh ; enveloped—as Ricord expresses it—in a kind of hard, circumscribed nucleus, which serves it both for a covering and a bed ; it has good claims for being called the most characteristic lesion of syphilis at its commencement.

4. Its isolation, being seldom or never accompanied by others of a like kind ; consequently its non-power of inoculation.

5. Its power of creating a series of sympathetic buboes in the groins, which seldom suppurate.

6. Finally, its power to resolve itself into constitutional symptoms of a loathsome and painful character, to be described hereafter.

GANGRENE and PHAGEDÆNA are almost the only complications attending a primary syphilitic sore. The former usually appears in the course of the ulcerative stage. The surface of the chancre, previously *red* or *greyish*, deepens in colour, and is dotted with dark points of ecchymosis ; there is increased pain, and a sanious secretion which contains the remains of tissue, and shreds of blackish blood ; the sore spreads and gradually destroys the surrounding hardened tissues. The latter presents a more or less irregular shape, with livid, jagged edges, a base slightly hardened, and œdematous ; an uneven floor, which is covered with a yellow or greyish matter, or sanious pus. Its tendency is to spread superficially rather than deeply, and there is generally a smarting or burning pain.

CAUSES.—The abuse of spirituous liquors in warm seasons, hot climates, unhealthy dwelling-places, bad food, want of cleanliness, the abuse of mercury, and various unhealthy and cachectic conditions of the body, may be set down as some of the chief causes of such complications.

TREATMENT.—The first manifestations of the great syphilitic epidemic of the fifteenth century—" of which the hard ' Hunterian chancre ' of the present day is a descendant and true representative," having been a complete surprise for the physicians of that remote period—were not treated at all. It was, in fact, considered disgraceful for a practitioner to occupy himself with such a disease. But it should be observed that the chief cause of such neglect was attributed more to ignorance of the nature of the complaint than to anything else.

" The learned," writes Gaspard Torella in 1500, " avoided treating this disease, being persuaded that they knew nothing about it; for since this strange disease had never been seen up to our time, no one, however clever, however experienced he might be, could treat it according to the rules of art." It was from this and other causes that the treatment of syphilis fell into the hands of druggists, herbalists, and various impostors of the healing art from that remote period even up to a very recent date ; and the remedies used were as singular as they were dangerous—such as *vipers* infused in wine, or made into broth, or syrup, or the flesh roasted or boiled. To these we may add the marrow of *deer, foxes, human fat, Venice soap*, and a decoction of *henbane*, &c. ; and in China, a decoction of *toads*.

The physicians in Germany at the first outbreak of the epidemic were quite as remiss as those of Italy, for Lawrence Phrisius, a physician at Mentz, in a discourse entitled *De Morbo Gallico*, cap. 1, 1532, says that "at first the poor people who were infected with this distemper were expelled from human society like a putrid carcass ; and being forsaken by the physicians (who would neither give their advice about them nor visit them), they dwelt in the fields and woods ;" and at last, says Astruc (chap. vi., p. 140), "the disease spreading wider than can well be imagined, and the number of such as wanted assistance increasing daily more and more, the physicians grew ashamed of neglecting their duty in so grievous a scourge, and thus medicine was first applied, and a cure attempted, rather through a sense of shame than any confidence of success." Guided by the theoretical views of the time, several eminent physicians agreed to a method of cure which they called *Methodical* or *Rational*.

Firstly, they ordered a spare diet according to the 9th aphorism of Hippocrates, consisting of food easy of digestion.

Secondly, bleeding, both generally and locally, by means of *leeches* and *cupping*.

Thirdly, mild laxatives, composed of *cassia, senna, manna, tamarinds*, and syrup of apples, *succory*, and *roses*.

Fourthly, they endeavoured to purify the blood by means of the juice of wild *succory, bugloss, spleenwort*,

H

asparagus, parsley, horehound, and the tops of *hops,* with syrups composed of the same juices. For the same purpose they prescribed warm baths, either alone or boiled with *marsh-mallows, water lilies, chamomile, linseed,* or the roots of the *wild cucumber.*

Fifthly, for pustular eruptions they recommended liniments of *mastic, myrrh, soot, quicksilver,* and *orris root,* first reduced to a fine powder ; and for bone pains hot oils, containing *laurel, chamomile, dill, spike,* and *saffron.* In obstinate cases they recommended sweating in *stoves,* or even in a moderately *hot oven,* and, according to Gaspar Torella, with good success ; for says that author, " Amongst all things which I had tried for curing the pains, and even the pustules, the best was to make the patient sweat in a *hot oven,* or *bagnio,* for five days successively in the morning fasting." Finally, they sometimes recommended cautery to the *head, arm,* and *leg,* with the view of letting out the latent reliques of the foul distemper."

From that period we are enabled to trace the use of a medicine which has become celebrated—and deservedly so — in the history of syphilis, namely, *Mercury*; the *Hydrargyrum* of the Greeks; the *Argentum Vivum* of the Latins; and the Mercurius of the more modern chemists.

Mercury was first introduced into the domain of therapeutics by the Arabian physicians, and recommended by Rhases to destroy vermin ; by Avicenna as a cure for the itch ; by Serapion for herpes ; and by Mesue as a cure for impetigo, the *Malum Mortuum,* " a form of lepra," and other cutaneous eruptions. Analogy naturally led to the employment of this drug for syphilitic eruptions, and, encouraged by earlier authorities, the first syphilographers followed therein the precepts laid down by Celsus, who says in his preface " that in case any unknown disease starts up, the physician must not therefore think of ordering out-of-the-way medicines ' by conjecture,' but must first consider what disease this new one is most akin to, and try remedies of the same sort with those which most frequently succeed in analogous diseases, and by such resemblance find out a proper method." At first *Mercury* was chiefly used externally, in the form of *liniment, ointment, cerate, fumigation,* and *lotion;* but it produced such terrible effects, particularly in the hands of illiterate persons, that the remedy soon became worse than the disease, and fell for a time into great discredit. This was materially hastened by the introduction into Europe in 1517 of the *guaiacum* or holy wood, a remedy largely used by the natives of Hispaniola in venereal affections. Few remedies became so rapidly popular ; but after a time this also fell into disrepute, from the supposition that it laid the foundation of diseases of the *lungs, liver, kidneys,* and *stomach.* " I have observed," says P. A. Matthiolus, in his Treatise *De Morbo Gallico,* pub. 1535, "that men of a dry habit of body, who are infected with the French disease, by drinking of this decoction fall into a hectic fever and consumption." Thus *guaiacum,* which at first was received with great applause, was obliged to give way to the *Cinchona officinalis,* introduced into Europe about the year 1535, and raised once more the expectations of both doctors and patients. To this succeeded *sarsaparilla, sassa-*

fras, juniper, millet, soap wort, burdoc, and the flesh of the *sea tortoise.*

In 1661 *opium* was introduced by S. Pauli, and in 1779 by other physicians, but with no satisfactory results. Towards the end of the last century *nitric acid* was advocated by Girtanner, Scott, and others, but this also underwent the same fate as others.

Gold, silver, brass, platina, Arsenic, Iodine, and the *Iodide of Potass* have likewise had their day, but, with the exception of the latter, have not stood the test of experience in the primary form of syphilis. Such is a brief outline of the " therapeutics " connected with the history of the great epidemic of 1494-5. Let us now to the more immediate object in view, viz., the *Homœopathic* or *Specific* treatment of the divers forms of chancre; for the rapid and successful treatment of which, it may safely be affirmed that there is no class of medicines contained in the wide range of either the allopathic or homœopathic materia medica, that can for a moment compete with the various compounds of *Quicksilver,* administered in potencies varying from the first to the sixth decimal dilutions, such as the *Merc. sol. Hah.; Merc. vivus; Merc. præc. rub.; Merc. bichloride; Merc. iod.; Merc. nitros;* and *Merc. phosph.;* selected with due regard to the form, stage, and condition of the chancre, its accompanying complications, and the constitutional peculiarities of the patient.

1. *The Dry Papule.*—Thirteen cases of this type have come under my notice; two of recent origin; they were treated with *Merc. sol. Hah.,* first and second decimal trituration, three grains twice a day: the callosity of one disappeared in four weeks, the second entirely

within five weeks, and left no *secondaries* behind. The remaining cases were first treated allopathically, and terminated in *secondaries*, which yielded to *Aur. met.* and *Hep. sulph.* This form requires no outward application.

2. *Chancriform Erosion*—which is by far the most frequent form of primary syphilis. Fifty-six cases of this type are recorded in my case books. In the majority of these I found the *Merc. præc. rub.* to be the best preparation in the ordinary type, in the second decimal trituration; others, which looked angry, with a tendency to spread, yielded to *Merc. corr.* 3x, and *Nitric acid*, first decimal trituration, in drop doses; and others, which assumed more of the Hunterian form, yielded well to Hahnemann's solution of Mercury, in the first and second trituration.

Outward applications here are very necessary, but they must be of a soothing nature. The well-known black wash and Tannic Acid I find far too irritating, but a combination of *Calendula, Carbolic acid,* and *Gum-water* act admirably. In some, where great irritation and sensibility existed, with threatened suppuration of the inguinal glands, I found it necessary to apply a poultice composed of *chamomile* and *poppy-heads,* which had a very soothing effect, reducing the inflammation, and setting up a more copious discharge, to the great relief and comfort of the patient. The duration of cure varied from four weeks to two months. Twelve of these cases terminated in *secondaries,* but of a mild form, and yielded chiefly to *Iodide of potass, Biniodide of mercury,* and *Turkish baths.*

3. *Indurated or Hunterian Chancre.*—In this form

of chancre, says Jahr, the leading remedy is and
always will be *Merc. sol. Hah.* Half a grain of the
centesimal trituration, given morning and evening,
will in most cases prove sufficient to effect a cure.
Seventy-five cases of true *Hunterian chancre*, as
recorded in my note-books for the last few years,
enables me to confirm these views to a great extent;
but there are some cases which will require the help
of other preparations of mercury to establish a radical
cure. "A chancre," as Vehsemeyer very justly says,
"exhibits in its course two stages, viz., an *ulcerative*
and a *reproductive* stage. The character of the first
stage is, *loss of substance*, the second, *adventitious
growth*. The syphilitic ulcer, if attacked on its very
first appearance, leaves this stage under the persistent
use of *Merc. sol.* in from twelve to fourteen days, in
doses of one to five grains of the *second* or *third*
decimal trituration, repeated three times a day. On
the sixth or eighth day an improvement becomes
apparent; the ulcer is arrested in its course; the
tenacious lardaceous substance which covers its floor,
like a false membrane, becomes eliminated or absorbed, and is replaced by a healthy secretion ; granulations form, the callosity gradually diminishes, the
edges drop in, and cicatrization takes place from the
circumference towards the centre, leaving for a time a
dark brownish bronze colour, which after a longer period
terminates in a white mark. But if this change does
not, from various causes take place within the time
indicated, another remedy should be selected. It may
be that the ulcer will assume a tendency to spread, in
such a case the *Merc. corr.* is well indicated ; or it may

assume an indolent form ; then *Merc. phosph.* will be found the most appropriate remedy. Other cases will sometimes occur, that instead of becoming cleansed from the circumference, the cleansing process of the ulcer proceeds from the centre ; the edges then become raised, grow like *condylomata,* and heal rapidly under the influence of the foregoing medicines ; and the second stage, or what has already been stated as "adventitious growth," set in, which should be combated by *Nitric acid,* two or three drops of the second dilution in water three times a day, and a weak solution of the acid or *Alum* externally.

Nitric acid is likewise a very valuable remedy in those cases of syphilis which attack scrofulous and broken-down constitutions, where mercury in any form save the *Iodide* would act most injuriously. In such cases, however, I do not hesitate to prescribe the compound of *Mercury* and *Iodine,* and have never found it act injuriously on such constitutions.

OUTWARD APPLICATIONS.—Strict cleanliness with tepid water frequently suffices for the treatment of infecting chancre. Some recommend the black wash, in which I have no faith, as being too irritating ; others the yellow wash. Lancereux recommends washing the sore with spirit and water, and the application of tincture of *guaco,* and afterwards dressing with calomel ointment, of the following proportions :—*Opiate cerate* 30 parts, *Calomel* 1 part ; mix, and apply three times a day. I am in the habit of prescribing a lotion consisting of *Tinct. calendula, Carbolic acid,* and a weak solution of gum. This has a *soothing, cleansing,* and *disinfecting* effect. It destroys the lardaceous deposit which covers the floor of this *chancre*, and promotes healthy granulations, and a more normal secretion.

COMPLICATIONS OF CHANCRE—THEIR TREATMENT.

Gangrene, Phagedæna, Buboes, Phimosis, Paraphimosis, Gonorrhœa, and *Moist Warts* are among the chief complications of a contagious syphilitic chancre.

When a chancre assumes a *gangrenous* or *phagedænic* form I omit for a time all mercurial preparations, and administer *Arsenicum* in low potencies, one grain of the third decimal trituration, or five drops of Fowler's solution three or four times a day. Perfect quietude in the recumbent posture, soothing applications, a plain non-stimulating diet, plenty of ventilation, and strict cleanliness, will form the most judicious plan of treatment.

Chancre and Buboes.—The syphilitic poison in its passage through the inguinal glands frequently gives rise to inflammation and enlargement of these organs, which in many instances terminate in *suppuration* and *ulceration*. In the treatment we ought to be guided by the same principles as in the treatment of the primary sore, by continuing the *Merc. sol.* But if the buboes become intensely inflamed, and threaten to break, then I substitute the *Merc. præc. rub.*, or *Nitric acid.* And if suppuration becomes inevitable, I hasten the *bubo* to maturity by means of *Hep. sulph.* or *Silecia*, and, when ripe, open it from above downwards with a curved-pointed bistoury.

Chancre with Phimosis and Paraphimosis.—Strict
cleanliness, cold evaporating spirituous lotions, the
recumbent posture, an occasional dose of *Acon.* or *Bell.*
to subdue inflammatory action, and the repeated administration of *Merc. corr.* constitute the chief mode
of treatment I am in the habit of adopting in this
form of complication.

Chancre and Gonorrhœa.—In such complications great
cleanliness is strictly enjoined, with the administration
of *Merc. sol.* or *Merc. corr.*, and if considerable scalding
exists, with *chordee*, &c., I alternate the selected
mercurial preparation with *Cannabis sativa*, or *Cantharis.*

Chancre and Condylomata.—Here *Merc. sol.* may be
given, with an occasional alternating dose of *Thuja* or
Nitric acid. Some recommend clipping these warts
with a pair of scissors. I object to such treatment as
a useless piece of barbarism and unscientific blunder ;
for 1 have had no difficulty whatever in removing
them by a properly selected medicine ; viz. *Thuja,
Nitric acid*, or *Alum*, in the form of lotion.

PART IV.

BUBOES.

A BUBO may be defined as a swelling of the lymphatic glands, particularly those of the groin and axilla.

The venereal virus in its course through the inguinal glands frequently gives rise to inflammation and enlargement of them, which in many instances is followed by suppuration and ulceration. The *swelling, abscess,* or *sore* thus produced is termed a *bubo,* a name derived from the Greek (βουβῶν, the groin) ; though if a patient happen to have a primary venereal sore on one of his fingers, he might have a *bubo* just above the elbow, near the inner edge of the biceps muscle, or in the *axilla* ; so that a *bubo* does not always signify a disease in the groin, as the etymology of the word would imply. Lancereux objects to this term, as not being sufficiently lucid or correct; he, however, retains it on account of its antiquity, but gives preference to the word *Adenopathy,*[*] which indicates more exactly what organ is affected.

In the Middle Ages, and even in more ancient times, suppurating buboes, and the co-existence of abscesses in the groin with ulcers of the genital organs, were well known and clearly defined. Hippocrates, who flourished some 450 years before

* From the Greek ἀδήν, a gland.

the Christian era, in his third book on Epidemics, refers to "*defluxions* to the private parts ; *pustules, ulcers, abscesses,* and suppurations, mutilations of the *bones* and *nerves, baldness,* and falling off of the *beard ;* " finally, "*swellings in the groin,*" clearly showing that syphilis and its attendant evils was well known at that remote period. Galen, A. D. 200, confirms the views of Hippocrates. In 1270, William de Salicet of Placenza, writes thus :— " This disease is called a *bubo, dragoncelli,* or *impostume* of the groin, which sometimes proceeds from a hot humour, and sometimes it comes upon a foulness in the yard (*in virga corruptio*) contracted by lying with a *slovenly* woman." Lanfranc of Milan, about the same time refers to these *impostumes* in the groin arising from ulcers of the yard. In 1470, Peter de Argelata, of Bologna, in describing venereal ulcers on the penis, also refers to buboes in the groin, which, if they suppurate, carry off the disease ; in 1532, Nicholas Massa to ulcers on the yard, which are obstinate with callous hardness, followed by "tumours in the groin." Paracelsus in 1536, Jerome Fracastorius in 1546, and, more particularly, Anthony Gallus in 1540, are very clear upon this point. " It sometimes happens," says the latter, "when the disease is confirmed, that a virulent humour appears in the groin, in the form of a hard boil, besetting as it were the glands, called ἀδίναι. This some call a *bubo,* others *pulinus* (a colt), by way of sneer, because they who are thus afflicted straddle with their legs as if they were riding on a colt."

Gaspard Torella appears to be the first who gave a

description of an affection of the lymphatic system
concomitant with the indurated or Hunterian chancre.
Starting from that period, buboes continued to be
described by most syphilographers up to the present
time. Thus, Astruc, in 1754, describes syphilitic buboes
as hard, resistent tumours of the lympathic glands of
the groin, which do not readily suppurate, and are
produced mediately or immediately from an impure
connection.

"Therefore when this species of *venereal* happens
either to man or woman, immediately from impure
coition, in a few days, few or more glands, in either
or both groins, give some small pain in walking, and if
you handle them, you may observe them to be enlarged.
The tumour increases by degrees, and grows hard
and tense; hence the part has a more acute sense of
pain and heat, but still retains its natural colour; the
patient by degrees finds more difficulty in walking;
at length a manifest bubo appears, various in its figure,
viz., *jorbicular*, *oblong* or *round;* sometimes of the
size of a pigeon's or hen's egg, sometimes as large as
one's fist." Finally, Ricord, Lancereux and others, like
the ancient physicians, draw a prominent line between
the sympathetic or virulent bubo of the *chancroid* or
soft sore, and the hard indolent bubo which accompanies
the *indurated* or *Hunterian* chancre—a distinction
which is recognised more or less by most modern
syphilographers. For all practical purposes buboes
may be set down under the following heads, viz.,—

1. Simple or sympathetic buboes.
2. Gonorrhœal buboes.
3. The virulent, inoculable buboes of soft chancre.

4. The indolent, multiple, indurated, non-inoculable, or true syphilitic buboes.

5. The phagedænic buboes.

Simple or *Sympathetic Buboes.*—The generality of buboes of this type, and not strictly venereal, are preceded and accompanied by more or less disorder of the general health. They constitute the "*bubo at the first outset*" of John Hunter, and the *bubon d'emblee* of the French. Diday, after a critical examination of the theory of buboes *at the first outset*, admits on the strength of a considerable number of cases, that these lesions have no *virulent character ;* that their incubation is long, and their duration about a month ; they are accompanied by an inflammation which is always slight, and a feverishness and feeling of discomfort comparatively intense ; they are connected in many cases with excessive coition, and similar to such as are observed in soldiers after long, fatiguing, and forced marches; or wounds lying in the track of lymphatics leading to the inguinal glands. Whenever a patient consults me for a swelling in the groin, who denies having ever contracted a sore of any kind on his penis, traces of which cannot be discovered by the most searching inquiry or the closest examination, I invariably lay it down as a rule—first, to inquire into his general state of health ; and, secondly, to ascertain whether there is any *inflammation, wound, boil, carbuncle,* or *sore* about the *foot, leg, thigh* or *nates ;* any *bunion* on the great toe, or any inflamed *bursa,* or painful *corn;* for it cannot have escaped the observation of any practitioner of moderate experience that the inguinal glands are liable to sympathetic inflammation and enlargement from any of these causes. Buboes of this type generally affect the deep-seated glands ; their progress is usually slow, with but little tendency to suppuration.

In the treatment of such buboes we must in a great measure be guided by the exciting cause ; remove this, the other naturally follows ; strike at the root, the branches fall and wither.

Gonorrhœal Buboes.—For the symptoms, causes, and treatment of buboes of this type see " Complications of Gonorrhæa," page 54.

Virulent, Inoculable, Non-infecting buboes of Soft Chancre.—The soft chancre, says Lancereux, most commonly runs through all its periods without exciting any sympathy in the inguinal glands. In a certain number of cases, however, *sixty-five* times in 207 cases (according to the statistics collected by Ricord) there supervenes in the course of this lesion, or soon after its appearance, acute *adenitis,* essentially *monoglandular,* which almost always runs on to suppuration, and furnishes a *virulent* pus which is inoculable like that of the chancre which caused it. Soft ulcers of the *frænum,* the *prepuce,* and *meatus* are, by virtue of the great number of lymphatic vessels with which those regions are supplied, especially disposed to the development of this form of bubo. Although it may occur at any period of the existence of the chancre, yet it does not usually show itself before the end of the first week, the chancre being lined, up to that time, by an inflamed tough tissue, which to a great extent prevents the absorption of the matter. The inflammatory process in the gland generally proceeds with great rapidity, and almost invariaby ends in suppuration.

DIAGNOSIS.—The form of bubo under consideration is not difficult of recognition, chiefly on account of the usual nature of the surrounding walls of the focus of suppuration and neighbouring parts. We likewise observe that instead of contracting gradually, and showing a tendency to heal (as in a simple sympathetic bubo), the opening spreads, and in many cases to considerable dimensions, burrowing under the sound skin, and secreting a serous or bloody pus. Another diagnostic sign worth recording is the anatomical range of the swelling ; for if we find one gland only affected, and that situate above Poupart's ligament, we are led to infer that it is of venereal origin ; but if a series of glands are swollen, and they are located below the margin of that ligament, the probability is that it is caused by some irritation in the lower extremity. The most frequent complication of a virulent bubo is undoubtedly *phagedæna*, the ravages of which in some cases are so frightful, that the muscles, vessels, and nerves are laid bare, the limbs deprived of their cutaneous covering, and the patient worn out by a suppuration at times most difficult to check. Such are the leading characteristics of a bubo connected with a soft chancre.

TREATMENT.—Venereal swellings of the inguinal glands are more dreaded by patients than any other form of venereal disease, and this terror is to a very great extent justified by the torturing mode of practice adopted by many practitioners of the allopathic school, such as *leeches, blisters, purgatives, cauterization*, and the like. The buboes of soft chancre are not as a rule attended by any great pain or inconvenience,

and patients so affected are able from first to last to
get about and attend to their ordinary avocations.
The remedies best adapted are those selected for the
chancre itself; such as *Nit. ac.*, *Ars. causticum*, and
the *Potassio-tartrate of Iron*; and it sometimes happens
that these remedies act so powerfully that a bubo
runs through the ordinary stages to suppuration and·
heals again before a complete cure of the chancre is
effected.   I have met with six cases of this kind.   On
the first indication of swelling in the groin the patient
should remain quiet and seek the recumbent posture
the greater part of his time ; cold water pledgets or a
cold spirit lotion should be applied to the affected
region ; the sore on the penis should be kept strictly
clean by bathing or syringing it three or four times a
day with tepid milk and water, to which may be
added a few drops of carbolic acid or Condy's fluid ;
and if much irritation exists, with a tendency to spread
or creep along, I have observed great benefit to follow
the application of emollient poultices, such as *carrot*,
marsh-mallow, or *bran*, and in some cases a lotion consisting of *Calendula*, *Carbolic acid*, and solution of
Gum arabic.   The chief object in view is to blunt the
sensibility and check the spread of the sore, for the
larger it gets the larger the number of lymphatics
become implicated ; the direct source of communication between the chancre and neighbouring glands.
Should suppuration, however, take place, in spite of
these preventive measures, I hasten its maturity by lin-
seed-meal poultices, *Hep. Sulph.*, or *Silecia*, and as soon
as the abscess points, I open it with a curved pointed
bistoury.   The destruction of tissue is then incon-

siderable, the wound small and clean, and under favourable circumstances healthy granulations spring up, which fill the cavity to the surface of the skin. But if the matter be allowed to accumulate until it finds its way to the surface, or until the skin is deeply and extensively implicated, or the abscess is opened by means of *caustic* or *potassa fusa*, a practice recommended by many eminent surgeons ; then a large, ragged, irregular wound is established, followed by extensive sloughing of the adjacent parts ; for it must always be borne in mind that the tendency of a soft sore is to SPREAD, EAT, and DESTROY, its power of re-inoculation being so remarkable, that wherever pus is deposited there a chancre is produced.

In ordinary cases of suppurating buboes the *Nitric acid* or *Potassio-tartrate of Iron* both internally and as a lotion will suffice ; the first or second decimal of the former, and Ricord's formula of the latter, viz., distilled water 250 parts ; potassio-tartrate of iron 30 parts ; three tablespoonfuls to be taken daily. The sore to be dressed three times a day with lint dipped in the same solution ; but I myself prefer, as an outward application, a combination of *Calendula, Carbolic acid*, and *Gum-water*.

The chief complication of a soft sore is *phagedæna*, which is not only a troublesome but a dangerous form, and demands the most prompt and careful management, both locally and constitutionally. It is chiefly to be met with in scrofulous, debilitated, and broken-down constitutions. The chief remedy is undoubtedly *Arsenicum*, which should be administered in the second or third decimal, or in the form of Fowler's solution.

I

In a case of *gangrene* of the penis, with bubo in the right groin, which came under my notice three years since, I obtained brilliant results from the *Secale cornutum*, second dilution, with a lotion of the same preparation as an outward application.

Mercury, in any form, I have no faith in, as it rather tends to aggravate the disease than otherwise. In extensive sloughing and rapid destruction of surrounding tissues it will sometimes be found necessary to apply the actual cautery.

Cooper recommends a combination of *Opium* and *Nitric acid*; Collis, the strong *Muriate of Antimony*; others, a strong solution of *Nitrate of Silver*; a caustic solution of *Iodine, Potassa fusa*, or undiluted *nitric Acid*. In one case of *gangrene*, and two cases of *phagedæna*, recorded in another part of this work, one application of *Nitric acid* sufficed to check the onward march of the enemy. Since then I have witnessed the most gratifying results to follow the prolonged use of cold sitz baths, both in the *corroding* and *phagedænic* forms of chancre and buboes. The patient's powers should be well sustained by a nourishing and generous diet, such as fresh milk, well-made cocoa or beef tea for breakfast ; boiled or roast mutton, with a glass or two of *Carlowitz* or *Ofen auslese* for dinner ; and a proportionately nourishing meal in the evening. He should be kept quiet, free from all care, and recline as much as possible in the recumbent posture.

INDOLENT, MULTIPLE, INDURATED, NON-INOCULABLE, SPECIFIC, OR TRUE SYPHILITIC BUBOES.

Unlike the *monoglandular* suppurative adenitis of *soft* chancre, the *indolent* and *indurated* buboes of true syphilis present themselves in the form of a series of small tumours not larger than filberts which stud one or both inguinal regions, and seldom suppurate. They are constant attendants on primary syphilis, appearing almost contemporaneously with or during the first or second week of the initial lesion. At first there is simply a slight glandular tension, which gives but little pain, and is scarcely recognised by the patient himself ; but when more developed they feel like so many rounded or oval, resistent, elastic, movable balls, which recall to the finger that presses them the sensation conveyed by that peculiar induration indicative of a true *Hunterian chancre*. They are generally of the same size, but sometimes a larger one appears in the centre, around which other glands of smaller size form, like so many satellites. This gland sometimes suppurates, but the abscess quickly heals, and the matter is *not inoculable*. This form of bubo is remarkable for its *tenacity*, and outlives in the majority of cases by months and even years the original chancre. This important circumstance, as Lancereux very justly observes, is not devoid of practical utility, as it may put us on the track of concealed or unrecognised constitutional syphilis. Resolution then is the usual termination of true syphilitic buboes, suppuration being only observed *five* times in thirty-three cases. Specific buboes are in themselves without serious inconveniences, but it must not be forgotten that they represent a sure sign of a True Syphilitic Infection.

TREATMENT.—Jahr very justly remarks that a bubo should, no more than a chancre, be treated with *cauterizing* or *desiccating* agents, if we desire to avoid the danger of seeing secondary constitutional syphilis break out in its place. The only external applications necessary are warm poultices, and these only when the inflammation becomes too painful, or when suppuration has taken place, with the view of hastening that process and bringing the abscess to a point ; consequently general treatment in the majority of cases suffices for combating the *adenopathies* of syphilitic chancre, and the remedies should be selected from that class termed *Mercurial*, as being the only true specifics against that particular form of venereal disease. All schools are more or less agreed upon that point. "For my part," writes Ricord, " a well-marked induration suffices to cause me to prescribe a general treatment, and from the first day on which I can discover it, I attack the diathesis point-blank." "Against the indurated or Hunterian chancre," writes Diday, "give mercury (the proto-iodide by preference). Homœopathic physicians, from the founder to the present time, are more or less in favour of the *Merc. sol. Hah.*, which alone suffices in a large proportion of cases. But it may be that some cases will assume the gangrenous or phagedænic form. for which *Arsenicum* should be selected. Others become aggravated through a scrofulous taint, when the *Biniodide of Mercury*, *Nitric acid*, or the *Iodide of Potassium* may be advantageously prescribed. For old indurated buboes, *Carbo animalis*, *Hep. sulph.*, and the *Iodide of Potass.* ; and for mismanaged buboes and constitutions already impregnated with allopathic doses of mercury, *Aurum metallicum*, *Nitric acid*, and *Hepar sulph.*, will prove our best friends.

LYMPHANGITIS. — The lymphatic vessels which

serve as a channel of communication between the
chancre and the inguinal glands sometimes become
affected with the syphilitic poison.   It is characterized
by the presence of small, hard, indolent, knotty cords,
which are swollen at some points and follow the
course of the lymphatic vessels ; they are movable
under the skin, and remain more or less sound in
their locality.   The course of lymphangitis is slow,
and its duration continues for several months.   It
generally terminates in resolution ; seldom in suppuration, except when some complication exists with
the initial lesion.

TREATMENT.—Similar to that of the buboes.

DIAGNOSIS AND PROGNOSIS OF SYPHILITIC AND
SYPHILOIDAL DISEASES.

Before we proceed to consider the remaining
sections of this monograph, it may be as well
to recapitulate briefly the *diagnosis* and *prognosis*
attending the initial forms and lesions of venereal
diseases. This, for brevity's sake, we shall endeavour to arrange in a tabular form, as being more
in accordance with the general programme of the
work, and more convenient as an index for reference ;
for it is not enough, as Lancereux very justly remarks,
to distinguish syphilis from what may simulate it.   It
is of vital importance, both for the patient as well as
the practitioner, to be able to know how to distinguish
true syphilis from *false* syphilis—the constitutional initial lesion from the purely local one ; for it is upon such
knowledge that a proper line of treatment can be laid
down for each particular case.   In this respect the

following table, which sums up the chief characteristics of each morbid condition, may not be without its use:—

TRUE SYPHILIS.
Primary lesion. Hunterian chancre.

INCUBATIVE STAGE.—A mean duration of twenty-seven days.

LESION.—Mostly *single*, and not re-inoculable on the subject of it.

CHARACTERISTICS OF SORE.— First consisting in a *papule* of greater or less size, which erodes or ulcerates, always forming a superficial ulcer, without detachment of the edges, and without suppuration, unless it be during the period of cicatrisation. In form, round or oval; base *hard* or *cartilaginous*, with tendency to dip down.

BUBOES.—Always accompanied by a series of *firm, indolent, non-suppurating* buboes in one or both groins, which sometimes suppurate; pus *not inoculable*.

GENERAL CONDITION OF THE SYSTEM.—A feeling of uneasiness, fatigue, lassitude, unusual weakness, vague pains, palpitations, a marked discolouration of the skin, a sensation of restlessness, melancholy, and a bellows murmur in the carotids.

BLOOD.—The red globules diminishing in quantity, the *albumen* proportionately increased.

CONSECUTIVE PHENOMENA.— Secondary, *tertiary*, and *visceral* lesions frequently result from a true Hunterian chancre.

COMPLICATIONS. — Gangrene, phagedæna, phymosis, and paraphymosis, rare.

TREATMENT.—Amenable to the influence of *mercurial* and *iodine* compounds.

PSEUDO, OR FALSE SYPHILIS.
Chanroid, or soft chancre.

Nil, or from a very few hours, to two days.

Many, and indefinitely re-inoculable on the subject of it.

First shows itself in the form of a vesiculo-pustule, then terminates in an ulcer more or less deep, with detached perpendicular edges, furnishing an abundant purulent secretion. In form irregular, base soft, with a tendency to spread *superficially*.

Accompanied in some cases only by buboes, which freely suppurate and furnish *inoculable* pus.

None.

No change; blood remains pure

None.

More general, and accompan at times by pultacious or di theritic deposit.

Entirely unaffected, and s times considerably aggravate the same remedies.

PROGNOSIS.

The question of prognosis is another point worthy of our best and closest consideration. The existence of true syphilis having been recognised, what leading indications are there which would enable us to form a correct prognosis as to whether the attack will be a severe or a mild one?   In other words, is there a kind of relationship existing between the form of the primary lesion, and the mildness or severity of the consecutive manifestations ?

This question, already considered by Carmichael and others, has been made by Bassereau the subject of many interesting researches, which have enabled him to form into a law the following indexes :—

1. Benignant or mild indurated chancres are followed by mild eruptions, and by affections of the various tissues, not tending to suppuration.

2. Phagedenic indurated chancres are followed by severe pustular eruptions ; ulcerating affections of the skin, suppurating exostoses, necrosis, and caries.

Diday, Bazin, Dubuc, Verneuil, and Langlebert are of opinion that a *true chancre* corresponds to severe syphilis ; a *chancriform erosion*, to a mild form.   The latter regards chancre as the touchstone of the constitution, and states that the benignity of the chancre will announce constitutional symptoms of little severity ; while its malignity, on the contrary, will lead us to expect consecutive symptoms of much greater severity.

PART V.

SYCOSIS.

ACCORDING to the programme laid down in the second section of this work, there remains a fourth species of the venereal disease to be added to those already described; namely, *warty* or *condylomatous* excrescences of the genitals, which sometimes succeed an impure coition, but more generally follow, and sometimes appear conjointly with chancre or gonorrhœa. The original nature of condyloma is, however, still a disputed point: some regard it as the products of *chancre*; others of *gonorrhœa*; while Hahnemann and many others contend that it springs from a peculiar poison of its own,—" *the sycosic miasm.*" But whatever may be said concerning the *syphilitic* or *idiopathically* sycosic nature of these excrescences, there is no disputing the fact of their being venereal; that is, products arising sooner or later from venereal infection, either as primary or consecutive phenomena, and endowed with the power of transmitting a like disease during the act of coïtion. Practically, however, such a distinction has no great value, as the history and symptoms of the complaint, "like the polar star," will lead the physician, "whether he recognises the former or the latter," to the selection of a proper remedy,—a great advantage enjoyed by homœopathy, but which allopathic physicians decline to recognise in their treatment of disease; merely in order to vindicate the dignity of a tottering system.

HISTORICALLY.—Venereal warts were first recognised and described by Peter Maynard, A.D. 1519, as follows :—" Wherefore I say that the chief sign of this disease [syphilis], as we see by experience, are *pustules* appearing on the extremity of the yard in men, and in the orifice of the vagina or neck of the womb in women. These pustules for the most part ulcerate: I say for the most part, because in some I have seen them hardening in the manner of WARTS, CORNS, and PORRI."

ANATOMICALLY, there are two kinds of sycosic excrescences which present themselves to our notice.

1: The GRAFTED, or IMPLANTED.—These are of greater density than that of the skin, to which they adhere by their base, or a sort of pedicle. Most of the sycosic products of this class are termed *fig-warts:* they are generally dry, or secrete but little.

2. HYPERTROPHIC EXCRESCENCES.—These arise by a simple swelling of the cellular tissue of a fold of the skin or mucous membrane—a kind of papillary hypertrophy : they quickly ulcerate, and secrete a fœtid, slimy pus.

Like syphilis, they first appear upon those parts that have received the contagion : in men upon the glans, the folds of the prepuce, and orifice of the urethra ; in women on the labia majora et minora, the clitoris, and around the urethra. If no impediment is put in the way of their growth, they rapidly increase in size and number ; if, on the other hand, they are destroyed by *caustic, amputation, strangulated by ligature*, or any other external appliances, the disease disappears from that place, but breaks out with greater vigour in another. We may then find them studding the *anus*, the *axilla*, the *fauces*, *lips*, *eyes*, or *tongue ;* indeed, there is scarcely any part of the body which is exempt from the invasion of these excrescences, once they are *ill-used, tampered with*, and driven back into the system.

In form they vary considerably : some are shaped like *cauliflowers ;* some like *warts ;* some like long stems or *goose-quills ;* and some like *raspberries, mulberries*, or *grapes ;* others are *fig-shaped*, and others assume the form of a *cockscomb*. These varieties in form depend in a great measure upon the shape, extent, and vitality of the organ or part originally infected. When for instance they appear on the corona glandis, or prepuce, they generally assume the form of stems or goose-quills ; if on the clitoris, and round the orifice of the urethra, they assume the form of a raspberry or grape, which are sometimes as red as the fruit itself. On the labia we meet with the cauliflower form ; animal vegetation, like the products of the earth, requires space and prolific soil for growth and development.

At the anus these vegetations accommodate themselves to the natural folds of the skin, and being flattened on either side, assume the characteristic form of the " crista galli," or cockscomb. Condylomata, whether *venereal* or *non-venereal*, most frequently attack persons who do not keep themselves clean, and on parts of the skin or mucous membranes where two *flat surfaces* come in contact with and rub against *each other*, from which corrosive secretions ooze out. They occur more frequently in females than in males.

But there is a considerable number of other derangements of nutrition dependent upon the same cause, which, strictly speaking, ought perhaps to come under the category of "secondary phenomena :" such as, for instance, the hypertrophy of the tonsils which follows syphilitic angina, and accompanied by mucous patches; the elongation and hypertrophy of the prepuce, with contraction of its opening after a chancre ; hypertrophy of the labia after the same cause, and also syphilitic contraction of the rectum.

TREATMENT.—From what has been said on the origin and pathology of condyloma, it must be evident to the most ordinary mind that such excrescences cannot be eradicated by mere outward manipulation, and surgical appliances. To recognise such an abortive system would be to eschew altogether the fundamental principles of pathology—the FONS ET ORIGOMALI, as well as the leading principles of homœopathy. "To remove a condyloma," says Cooper, "the practitioner may either destroy it with CAUSTIC, tie its base with a LIGATURE, or remove it at once with a KNIFE." A recent writer on the homœopathic treatment of venereal diseases adopts this ad captandum mode of treatment; for in describing a case of gonorrhœa with a " *luxuriant crop of warts encircling the anus*," he SNIPS them off with a pair of *scissors*, applies dry lint to the parts operated upon, and gives *Thuja* internally, "veni, vidi, vici."

A CONDYLOMA, be its cause or form what it may, is as amenable to homœopathic treatment as any other *disease I know of*; and, like the varied and multifarious eruptions on the skin surface, is simply an outward manifestation of some internal *dyscracy*, which will yield kindly enough to its specific remedy. A host of such cases may here be recorded ; but I forbear on the plea that such might be construed by some of my readers as *claptrap, sensational* cures.

Warts of a non-venereal or uncomplicated nature are best treated by *Causticum, Dulcamara, Rhus,* or *Thuja.*

Warts complicated with gonorrhœa, will in the majority of cases yield to the internal and external use of *Thuja.* It is in the power of the ARBOR VITÆ to produce—besides gonorrhœal affections—cutaneous excrescences on the parts of generation, and on other parts of the body, in the form of *tubercles* and *warts,* as secondary products. It was this which induced Hahnemann to regard *Thuja* as a specific in those condyloma which so frequently attend gonorrhœa. This has since been amply confirmed by the experience of Trinks, Mayrhofer, Warnatz, Hufeland, Rummel, Mohnike, Jahr, others, and myself.

The special therapeutic indications which point to the selection of *Thuja* are, *Gonorrhœa,* past or present ; *Leucorrhœa; Condylomata* on a broad base, and cracked; a *mulberry-shaped moist surface,* with itching and burning in the excrescences. *Lycopodium, Cinnabaris,* and *Sabina,* used externally and internally, have in many cases performed excellent cures.

Warts complicated, with the chancroid, or soft chancre, yield remarkably well to *Nitric acid* and *Causticum ;* and warts complicated with the hard Hunterian sore, to *Merc. sol., Merc. corr., Phosph. ac.,* or *Staphysagria.*

Some practitioners have the selected remedies in accordance with—

1. The form of the condylomata.

2. According to their locality when first manifesting themselves.

3. According to their origin on first appearing.

Thus for broad, flat, bean-shaped condylomata, they select *Thuja* and *Nitric acid.*

For elevated, cauliflower, raspberry, or mulberry-shaped, *Thuja.*

For fan-shaped, *Cinnabaris.*

For pedunculated, *Lycopodium* and *Nitric acid.*

For cone-shaped, *Merc. sol.*

When dry, *Thuja, Merc. sol., Merc. corr., Nitric ac.,* or *Lycop.*

When moist and suppurating, *Nitric ac., Thuja,* and *Sulph.*

When soft and spongy, *Sulph.*

When they appear on the glans or corona glandis, *Nitric ac., Thuja, Cinnab., Lycop.* and *Sulph.*

When on the prepuce, *Thuja, Nitric ac., Lycop.* and *Merc. corr.*

When on the scrotum, *Thuja.*

When on the anus, *Thuja* and *Merc. corr.*

After chancres, *Thuja, Merc. sol.,* and *Staphys.*

After gonorrhœa, *Thuja, Lycop.,* and *Cinnab.*

Hempel has found *Tartar emetic* a valuable curative agent when other remedies have entirely failed. He prescribes a lotion consisting of ten grains of the tartar emetic to four ounces of water; and the one-hundredth of a grain dissolved in eight ounces of water; a tablespoonful to be taken every four hours.

PART VI.

CONGENITAL SYPHILIS.

HISTORY.—Gaspar Torella in 1500, and Nicolas Massa in 1532, were about the first physicians who noticed at any length the hereditary form of syphilitic disease. "The hereditary diseases," write these men, "may be communicated to the fœtus by either of the parents, father or mother,—by the father as the seminal particles discharged from him, and fraught with the venereal venom, may infect the *embryo*, which they touch with the like disorder; and from the mother, as at the time she supplies the fœtus with nourishment during her pregnancy, she must convey into it the seeds of the distemper she labours under."* "Thus, from an infected mother," remarks another, "has been observed to come *squalid, semi-putrid, ulcerous*, and downright *venereal* births; nay, which is still more wonderful, by a venereal father have been begot ten infants actually venereal and ulcerous, though the mother was sound, or at least not affected with any manifest symptom of the venereal disease; as if the poison which destroys the tender body of the *embryo* was not strong enough to hurt the firmer habit of the mother." But hereditary syphilis, although partly recognised by these early syphilographers, has only been carefully studied since the close of the last century, by such men as

* Victor Trincavellus, Venice, 1561.

Doublet, Desmarres, and Diday in France ; Babington, Hutchinson, and others in England.

Hereditary syphilis, then, is that form of the specific disease in infants which is acquired during the period it tarries in the womb, *intra-uterine life*. It is necessary for practical purposes to make this distinction ; for when the complaint has contaminated the system after birth, it runs the same course even in the youngest children as in adults. The possibility, but not the probability of infection *in transitu* from the womb is clearly admitted; but neither of syphilis thus contracted, nor of it when imbibed during *lactation*, nor of it when transmitted by *vaccination* or any other accidental cause, do we now speak.

Congenital or hereditary syphilis may be either due to both parents, to father alone, or mother alone, having had at the time of conception the morbific taint circulating in their, his, or her system,—or, conception having taken place, the mother acquires the disease and infects her offspring. It is by no means necessary that there should be any outward manifestation of that terrible affection in either of the parents ; would that it were ! for then one of the most fruitful causes of *abortions* and infantile mortality might be stamped out, or at all events very considerably lessened. Now alas ! the poisonous and all-destructive seeds of the malady may lie dormant for months, and even years, unsuspected, and yet all-powerful to break forth in augmented fury in proportion to its lengthened quiescence. The period of the first appearance of the hereditary taint varies considerably, but the more virulent it is, the sooner it appears. A certain number of

children succumb at an early period of growth in their
mother's womb ; others come into the world with
unmistakable lesions of a syphilitic type ; but the
majority of cases at birth show no signs whatever of
so foul an inheritance, and matters go on as merry as
a marriage bell. Thus a child may exhibit no
symptoms of any *cachexia* at first, but during a period
varying from a few days to two or three months, is
noticed to present a *miniature picture of decrepitude*,
as Doublet has it. This stage of the disease may end
in death, or pass on to another. The countenance
then puts on a peculiar colour and expression ; there
is difficulty of breathing through the nostrils, a kind
of obstruction known as *snuffles*. "The face," says
Trousseau, "is of a peculiar sooty tint, as if a layer of
coffee grounds, or of soot mixed with a quantity of
water, had been passed over the features." An
earthy complexion with a peculiar cadaverous odour,
cracks, fissures, and condylomata show themselves
around the *mouth, nose, eyes*, and *anus ;* the eyebrows
and lashes drop off, and the eyelids are frequently
reversed. Roseolar, papular, vesicular, pustular, ecthy-
matous, tubercular, and scaly eruptions appear on the
skin. Iritis, interstitial keratitis, choroiditis, and
amaurosis affect the eyes; vomiting, thrush, a frequent
and obstinate diarrhœa, with sometimes bloody stools,
affect the alimentary canal; and insomnia, coma, con-
vulsions, epilepsy, paralysis, and hydrocephalus may
affect the brain. The child may survive these, or some
of these phenomena if not injudiciously treated, and
survive till the period of puberty, when a desperate
struggle now appears to take place for the mastery,

between the disease and the constitution ; and either death may claim its victim, or retarded growth, or one or more of the numerous morbid phenomena, such as deafness, blindness, idiotcy, disease of the liver, kidneys, or an affection of the skin of peculiar severity and extreme obstinacy set in.

PROGNOSIS.—The more nearly to birth that the symptoms develop themselves, by so much the more unlikely it is that the patient can be cured.

Trousseau has never seen an infant recover when the disease appeared within a few days after delivery. Children who are not attacked till they are two or three months old usually recover, under judicious treatment, a fair degree of health in a short time ; but the complete eradication of the *cachexia* requires a prolonged administration of carefully selected *anti-psorics*, and a well-regulated hygienic treatment.

When congenital syphilis manifests itself for the first time at adult age, it will generally be amenable to medication, particularly if attacked before permanent disorganization has taken place.

DIAGNOSIS.—The disease will, when it has once been seen, never be forgotten. The poison so thoroughly permeates the whole system, attacks mucous membranes, the skin, the glandular and osseous structures, as to give unmistakable evidence of its presence. The pathognomonic symptoms are, however, met with in the *mucous membrane* of the *nose*, and in the permanent incisor teeth of the upper jaw. The nasal mucous, or " *Schneiderian* " membrane, is attacked by inflammation, giving rise to the secretion of highly offensive mucus, and causing a

K

peculiar and characteristic *snuffling* noise. This inflammatory action but too frequently extends to the cartilaginous and osseous parts of the nose, and we see then the protuberant forehead and *snubbed nose*. The upper incisor teeth of the temporary set are prematurely lost, and the great *diagnostic* symptom of the disease is met with in the *permanent central upper incisors*, which are usually observed to be of a bad colour, short and peggy, round at the angles, standing apart, or converging, and marked by a deep notch.   Normally these teeth are chisel-shaped, that is broader at their cutting edges than at their insertions into the gum. The malformation indicative of congenital syphilis consists, firstly, in a reversal of the normal shape so far as this, that the two teeth above-named are *narrower* at their cutting edges than at their insertions into the gum ; hence their frequent comparison to "screwdrivers."   Secondly, the teeth are often notched ; hence such teeth are often called "notched teeth."   It is, however, important to bear in mind that Mr. Jonathan Hutchinson, to whose able researches on constitutional syphilis we owe this valuable diagnostic sign, has pointed out that it is rare to find teeth so malformed except in the eldest living of a syphilitic family, the exceptions being few.

TREATMENT.—*Congenital, transmitted,* or *hereditary syphilis* calls for treatment in the *fœtus,* in the *new-born child,* and at a more advanced period of life.   To combat the disease during *fœtal life,* medicines must be transmitted through the mother, *Merc. sol. Hah.* being one of the best preparations. A grain of the *first* or *second* decimal trituration should be taken night and morning for at least ten days or a fortnight, or even longer.

To attack the syphilitic diathesis in the *new-born child*, *Mercury*, *Iodide of Iron*, and *China* are our chief remedies. Various modes have been adopted by allopathic physicians for the administration of *Mercury*, which by common consent is looked upon as the most efficacious remedy extant. It has been transmitted through the mother's milk, through nurses, and through goats and asses. The idea of treating the disease in this way was first promulgated by the renowned physician of Cos, 450 B.C., and imitated by Garnion of Lyons in 1699, Burton in 1775, Doublet and many more at a more recent period; this was called the *indirect* treatment, in contradistinction to baths and inunction, termed the *direct* external mode of treatment. This mode of treatment has, however, long since fallen into disuse, as a course of strict chemical analysis failed to discover any traces of mercury in the milk of those animals.

Homœopathy, however, gives us not only a principle, but a mode of manipulation, which enables us to reduce our drugs to the smallest fractional dose without speculation, consequently they neither disturb the system, nor act injuriously upon the constitution. I am in the habit of commencing the treatment with a few doses of *Sulphur* 6. Not that that medicine has any specific control over the syphilitic poison, but it appears to me to render the system more susceptible to the action of the true specific; for I generally find an aggravation of symptoms to follow the administration of a few doses of that medicine, or a fresh crop of pustules to spring up, as if the latent powers of nature were roused to do battle against the common enemy with fresh energy. After this I administer one of the mercurial preparations, the *Merc. sol.* or *Bin-iodide* by preference, one grain of the second or third decimal potency night and morning, and a dose of *China* or *Iodide of Iron* two or three times a day. With these means, coupled with warm baths, vapour or Turkish baths, cod liver oil, and a well-selected, generous diet, I have been able to jog on remarkably well. Should, however, *Mercury* have been given allopathically before the case comes under notice, I antidote the ill effects of that drug by *Hep. sulph.*, followed up by *China, Iodide of Iron*, and cod liver oil, either by the mouth or the skin; and sometimes by *Nitric acid.* Dyspeptic symptoms should be removed by an occasional dose of *Nux vom., Puls.,* or *Sulphur.*

The ophthalmic derangements by *Merc. corr., Bell.,* and cod liver oil.

The ozæna by the *Iodide* or *Bichromate of Potassium,* and a weak solution of carbolic acid or Condy's fluid used as an injection.

The various eruptions on the body, constituting what may be termed the secondary phenomena, are best treated by one of the mercurial preparations, *Arsenicum* and *Sulphur,* and the deep-seated dyscrasia by *Aurum metallicum, Iodide of Potassium,* and cod liver oil. The diet should also be strictly attended to, and in every available manner we should seek to support the strength of the sad and innocent inheritor of youthful folly and parental crime.

PART VII.

CONSTITUTIONAL SYPHILIS.

HAVING now disposed of the main features connected with the primary form of Syphilis and syphiloidal diseases, together with their various complications, let us proceed briefly to review the constitutional ravages inflicted on the various tissues of the body by the foul invader known as—

1. *Secondary Symptoms*, or the period of general eruption.

2. *Tertiary* and *Quaternary Symptoms ;* otherwise known as the period of gummy products, and visceral lesions.

Instead, therefore, of appearing in the form of a simple local lesion—a chancre—true syphilis now begins to show, in its manifestations, the tendency to generalization, and to a multiplicity of morbid forms, whence it has justly received the name of "Proteus," which Fallopius, in 1560, was one of the first to give to it. We have already observed, in describing the leading characteristics of a "true Hunterian sore," that after a longer or shorter period of incubation there will appear on some part of the penis a minute spot or *papule*, gradually reaching the size of a lentil or pea ; that it is usually of a red or dirty yellow colour, ROUNDED and HARD to the touch ; that this papule becomes in course of time covered with greyish scales, which increase in thickness, and end by forming in most cases a true crust, under which a cup-shaped ulcer of greater or less depth rapidly develops itself, assuming at times a *serrated* or *sharp-edged* circular form, as if cut with a punch, the floor of which is lined by a greyish, *tough, lardaceous* secretion, which is *not re-inoculable*. The nature of this substance is of so stubborn a character as to resist every appliance at the command of the surgeon, its singular toughness not giving way to the most vigorous treatment until fairly established in the system. Indeed, the remedies adopted by most inexperienced pretenders only magnify and stimulate the formation to a far greater *obstinacy* and *virulence ;* the more it is outwardly attacked, as in some other complaints where *callosities* are presented, the greater force it displays in recruiting itself for a renewed onslaught on the already enfeebled constitution. This CHANCRE, which is a living representative of the great epidemic of the fourteenth century, may in truth be compared to a fortified citadel, possessing within its walls an almost inexhaustible store of ammunition and implements of destruction, whence a powerful garrison continually sallies forth to spread ruin and destruction throughout the whole frame. Having established itself during the period of incubation, it has thus returned to the surface from a searching expedition, and satisfied by this preliminary raid, its efforts are in future definitely directed from the surface as a radius against the subcutaneous tissues, the blood, muscles, bones, viscera, spinal marrow, and finally the brain itself. Its appearance in the system is first announced

by the development of febrile symptoms—syphilitic
fever—marked by an intense headache, pallor of the
countenance, a morose, taciturn, gloomy physiognomy,
a dark circle round the eyes ; erratic shooting pains
wander over the whole body, rigors alternating with
heats, followed by more or less perspiration, closely
resembling intermittent fever.   The pulse is quick,
and sometimes amounts to 110 or even 120 strokes to
the minute ; the digestive functions become deranged,
there is want of appetite, a bitter taste in the mouth,
nausea, and sometimes a diarrhœa ; the urine becomes
red and febrile, at the same time the patient feels a
lassitude and restlessness which unfit him for work.
The sense of fatigue and weakness is at times so great
that walking becomes irksome, the legs totter and
bend under the weight of the body, and neither bed
nor sleep affords the hapless sufferer either repose or
refreshment.   Following these symptoms we behold,
more or less in succession, on the surface of the body,
the palms of the hands, and the soles of the feet—
*erythematous, papular, pustular, vesicular, squamous,
pigmentary,* and foul *eczematous* eruptions—

> " And swift as quicksilver it courses through
> The natural gates and alleys of the body ;
> And with a sudden vigour it doth posset
> And curd, like eager droppings into milk,
> The *thin* and *wholesome* blood ;
> And a most instant tetter barks about
> Most lazar-like, with vile and loathsome crust
> All the smooth body."

It will destroy the hair of the head, the beard, eyebrows, and eyelashes, producing partial, and even
complete alopecia ; a symptom first noticed by Jerome

Fracastorius in 1546, and later on by Fallopius in
1560.

It will attack the epidermis of the scalp, face, beard,
eyebrows, and more specially the palms of the hands
and soles of the feet, in the form of a fine branny
desquamation, producing that disease known as
pityriasis.

ONYXIS.—It will attack the nails of the hands, feet,
and surrounding structures, rendering the former
wrinkled, brittle, distorted, and exfoliated ; the latter
ulcerated, presenting a fungous, moist brownish surface, which readily bleeds when touched, and furnishes
an ichorous and fœtid discharge ; a symptom which,
according to Brassavola, did not appear till about 1533,
some forty years after the first appearance of the great
epidemic.

It will invade the mucous membrane, and extend .
its ravages from the lips and nares to the vaginal and
anal regions ; developing in succession *erythematous
patches, papules, pustules, mucous patches, erosions, ulceration* and exfoliation of the *Schneiderian* membrane,
the inner surface of the lips and cheeks, the tongue,
uvula, tonsils, velum palati, pillars of the fauces, the
pharynx, larynx, vocal chords, trachea and bronchial
tubes, the œsophagus, stomach, and intestinal canal.

It permeates the glandular and lymphatic system,
and marks its presence by a firm elastic and swollen
condition of a series of glands in the cervical, inguinal,
and other regions, with a chord-like feel of the
lymphatic vessels.

It engenders a series of vegetations or glandular
hypertrophies, known as *sycosis, fig-warts,* and *condy-*

loma, which vary in form from a fan or cone to that of a grape, raspberry, mulberry, or cauliflower, which John de Vigo in 1519 was about the first to describe.

SYPHILITIC OPTHALMIA.—It will attack the various structures of the eye in the form of *iritis, choroiditis, retinitis, sclerotitis,* and *amaurosis ;* ulceration of the eyelid, and deposits in its appendages ; sties, warts, and other unsightly excrescences.

It frequently destroys the functions of hearing by setting up a papular or ulcerative process, which either thickens or breaks down the *tympanum* and *ossicula audita,* followed by an offensive sanious or ichorous discharge.

Various derangements of the organs of hearing were recognised at a very early period of the great outbreak of syphilis. Gabriel Fallopius, a native of Modena, in a discourse, *De Morbo Gallico,* 1540, says :— " Till within these ten years I never heard any mention of a noise in the ears which I can only compare to the sound of bells. I first observed it about eight years ago, and there are few now who have it not when the disease is quite confirmed. Observe this very diligently," adds he, " for you will not meet with it in other authors."

It will attack the various nerves that spring from the brain and spinal column, producing the most excruciating facial pains in some, partial or total paralysis in others.

PERIOSTITIS.—The bones do not always escape the attack of *secondary syphilis.* Those which are superficial, such as the tibiæ, the clavicles, and bones of the skull, are the most liable to them. They are affected

with pains of the most violent kind, fairly supportable
during the day, but sometimes intolerable during the
night, particularly from nine or ten p.m. to four or
five in the morning.

SECONDARY SYPHILITIC JAUNDICE. — Various
authors maintain that congestion, and it may be inflammation of the liver, terminating in jaundice, is
occasionally met with as a secondary phenomenon. It
was first observed by Paracelsus, and afterwards by
Garnier, Astruc, Ricord, and others. This form of
jaundice is not of great severity or of long duration,
and yields kindly enough to *Merc. sol.*, *Podophyllum
peltatum* or the *Iodide of Potassium*.

Thus have I endeavoured to enumerate the principal
features connected with that group of morbid phenomena termed *secondary symptoms;* and it will be
observed that the disease has hitherto confined itself
chiefly to surface and locality,—to the bark, so to
speak of the human tree ; but here it does not tarry
long unless confronted by well-selected medicines and
quickly eradicated from the system, but glides into
the—

Tertiary and *Quaternary* symptoms, known as the
period of *gummy products*, and *visceral lesions*. To
the transient and superficial changes described in the
above catalogue now succeed lesions of far greater
gravity, which do not spare the deep-seated structures
and viscera, any more than the common tegumentary
covering itself. It is now no longer, as Lancereux
says, simple *hyperæmia*, with or without exudation ;
inflammations, slight and of short duration ; but
profound changes, essentially slow in their evolutions

and marked by chronic inflammation, sometimes extensive and disseminated in a single organ, sometimes more limited and circumscribed. These changes appear in the form of *nodules* and *tubercles*, and it is then that the name of *gummy tumours* is more particularly reserved for them. In fact, while the lesions of the *secondary period* leave no appreciable trace behind, those of the *third* change or destroy more or less completely the organ or structure in which they exist, and frequently commit the most frightful and irremediable ravages.

On the skin there is now developed *pustules, tubercles, impetigo, ecthyma, rupia, lepra, cracks* and *fissures* which plunge deeply into the subjacent structures, having a greyish, dirty, purulent floor covered with thick, wrinkled, brownish or green crust, and surrounded by a copper-coloured margin. *On the head* we frequently encounter, in addition to *alopecia*, the deposit of *gummy tumours, phagedænic* ulceration of the scalp, and *necrosis* of the bony structure. On the fingers and toes we meet with deep-seated ulcers at their extremities, the nails become thickened, wrinkled and soft, and frequently fall off, leaving the ends of the phalanges in a state of *caries* or *necrosis.*

In the sub-cutaneous cellular tissue of the head, chest, shoulders, clavicular regions, and other parts of the body, we often meet with gummy tumours, which present themselves in the form of irregular masses varying in size from a *nut* or *walnut* to a *hen's egg*, and sometimes they stand alone.

In the mammary glands, the same abnormal structure is found deposited ; and it is to be regretted that the study of them has been hitherto incomplete and obscure ; for an exact knowledge of these morbid manifestations would permit, more frequently perhaps than is generally imagined, of substituting for an operation which carries with it no ordinary amount of'speculation and danger, a treatment certain and inoffensive.

Bones, Cartilages, and Joints.—The knowledge of syphilitic affections of the bones goes back as far as 1519, when John de Vigo thus described them in his " Practic. Chirurg.," lib. 5, cap. 1. :—" At the same time likewise with the above-mentioned *pustules*, or at least after their appearance, within six weeks or thereabouts, the patient was tortured with violent pains, sometimes about the forehead, sometimes in the shoulder-blades, and sometimes in the *shins, hips*, and *haunches.* A year or more afterwards there arose *scirrhosities* like bones, excessively painful, especially in the night-time, and easier in the day. The pain for the most part ended in corrupting the bone and marrow, after the same manner as it happens in the *spina ventosa.*" Tertiary syphilitic lesions of the bony tissue extend from the most simple form of inflammation of its outer covering to the most profound disorganization of the whole substance. Thus we find that the syphilitic poison will attack the bones in the form of *osteo-periostitis* and *exostosis*, which is a frequent result of the former ; also *gummy tumours*, which may occupy the periosteum or the medullary substance of the bone itself, as *caries, necrosis, atrophy*, or dry caries, *hypertrophy*, and *softening.*

GENITAL ORGANS IN THE MALE.—Like most

syphilitic lesions, the changes in the testicle in syphilis show themselves under two distinct forms; one *diffused*, the other *circumscribed*. The diffused consists of the deposit of fibrinous or tendinous bands, which traverse the whole or greater part of the organ and insinuate themselves between the seminiferous tubes. The testicle then becomes hard, swollen, and resistent. Pathologically, the whole organ undergoes a true fibro-fatty transformation.

The circumscribed form consists of the deposit of gummy products in the epididymis, or the substance of the testicles. The symptoms at first are somewhat obscure, in consequence of the absence of any particular pain, swelling, or redness. The leading indications are, a gradual increase in volume of the organ, which becomes heavy, hard, and firm to the touch. It is uneven, indurated, and communicates the sensation of an agglomeration of tumours, which are indented, rounded, and elastic. At other times it conveys the impression as if it were enclosed in a firm and resistent shell. There is little or no venereal desire. The functions of generation gradually become weakened ; erections occur with more, and more difficulty ; the secretion of semen diminishes, or may cease entirely, particularly if both testicles are diseased ; and hence the *impotence* and *sterility* so frequently connected with the existence of syphilitic orchitis.

The tongue, tonsils, velum palati, palatine arch, the pharynx and larynx become the seat of deep, perforating or *serpiginous* ulcers and *gummy tumours*.

Morbid anatomy, with the aid of the microscope, has revealed the startling fact that no organ or structure of the body, however minute, escapes the ravages of this foul invader. Follicular hypertrophy, excoriations, aphthous ulcerations, endometritis, and warty excrescences have been found in the vagina and uterus; atrophy and gummy tumours in the ovaries and fallopian tubes. Ulcerations and cicatrices are met with in the canal of the urethra, and tubercles in the corpora cavernosa. To be brief, gummy tumours, circumscribed syphiloma, lardaceous, amyloid, cirrhosis, and fatty degeneration are frequently found deposited in the heart, lungs, liver, pancreas, spleen, kidneys, and supra-renal capsules, the result of syphilitic poison.

Finally, neither is that great centre of the nervous system, the supposed citadel of the soul, proof against the destructive armaments of this fell destroyer. Gummy tumours and other syphilitic products have been found on the dura mater, the arachnoid, pia mater, and in the various chambers and hemispheres of the brain; causing in some severe and prolonged headache, in others the most painful form of neuralgia, insomnia, loss of memory, vertigo, dulness of mind, difficulty of speech, chorea, hemiplegia, paraplegia, general paralysis, epilepsy, and catalepsy in its worst and most hopeless form; in others, dementia, melancholia, and hallucinations. In fact, as Professor Griesinger very truly observes, " the mental derangements connected with syphilis present themselves under forms varying from the most *violent* MANIA, to the most complete IDIOTCY."

Such, then, is a very brief outline of the chief morbid phenomena met with in the *tertiary* and *quaternary* forms of true syphilis ; let us now to the—

TREATMENT.—" The chief therapeutic agent to oppose the manifestations of *secondary symptoms*," writes Lancereux, " is *Mercury*." " With a vesicular, squamous, or pustular syphilide," writes Diday, " give Mercury—the *bichloride*, *protochloride*, and *proto-iodide* by preference, particularly the first." This, to a great extent, has been amply confirmed by those eminent syphilographers, Cazenave, Ricord, Bazin, and many others. Numerous other preparations are in use, all of which contain quicksilver in some form or other ; such as the celebrated pills of Belloste, Sédillot, Cullerier, Dupuytren, Cazenave, and Ricord ; the drops of Van Swieten ; the mixture of Mialhe ; and the syrup of Larrey, Puche, and Gibert, for-mulas for each of which will be found at the end of this work. Such are the various preparations usually employed by the leading French physicians in the treatment of *secondary syphilis*, the bichloride by preference ; but a wide field of experience has taught them that it is sometimes necessary, for the purpose of obtaining a more rapid cure, to vary the preparations. " I have seen," says Bazin, "syphilides, favourably modified at first by the *protoiodide*, be-come stationary all at once, although the treatment was continued strictly, and only present a fresh tendency to resolution when another compound of Mercury was substituted for the *protoiodide*, such as Van Swieten's drops, or Dupuytren's pills." Bazin begins the treatment of the syphilides with a pill containing three-eighths of a grain of the *proto-iodide*, and asserts that "it is useless to give more than three quarters of a grain, seeing that no advantage is obtained from larger doses"—a very wise and judicious provision, coupled with a strong tendency towards homœopathy.

· Lancereux, in his very able work on syphilis, from the perusal of which I have derived much valuable information, particularly that section devoted to the constitutional ravages of the disease, puts this very important question,—" How long ought Mercury to be continued, and what indications follow to induce us to omit that medicine ? "

John Hunter was in the habit of giving a quantity of Mercury in proportion to the number of ulcerated surfaces and the violence of the disease. Dupuytren continued the treatment up to the complete extinction of the symptoms, *plus* a period equal to that required for the cure. Ricord says, " Six months of mercurial treatment, *plus* three months of treatment with preparations of Iodine, is the method which furnishes the most permanent cures ; and which succeeds, in an enormous majority of cases, in really neutralising the poisonous influence, and curing the syphilis."

Diday administers the mercurial preparations till the syphilides completely disappears, then omits it, but returns to it again should a fresh eruption appear. Bazin adopts a somewhat similar plan, but relies more on hygiene than therapeutics to eradicate the remnants of the disease, and restore the organism to *its normal* standard whenever relapses take place.

As a special remedy for secondary syphilis, Mercury does not on that account suit all cases. A bad condition of the primæ viæ, debility of the organism, and a certain degree of chloro-anæmia, are so many contra-indications which should be taken into account. "In persons of a delicate constitution, affected with scrofula, predisposed to phthisis and to other diseases of the same class, Mercury should not be given," says the late Sir Benjamin Brodie, "until it has been ascertained to be indispensable. But," adds the same observer, "I believe that scrofulous subjects who have a well-marked syphilitic affection are treated with more advantage by the aid of this medicine, for if the Mercury be deleterious for them, the syphilis is still more so." It is very evident from the foregoing remarks that the late Barandt was unacquainted with the safe and valuable properties of the compound of Mercury and Iodine which in my hands has proved eminently successful in constitutions savouring of the scrofulous taint. Individuals who have all the appearances of vigorous health are not always those who best support the preparations of Mercury. Those who are in the habit of drinking much, and who lead an irregular life, place their constitutions in a condition little favourable for the employment of those preparations; with them it is better to defer the use of Mercury until the constitution has been improved, so as to avoid having to combat, later on, both mercurial and syphilitic affections. Sometimes, for reasons which could not be foreseen, Mercury acts as a poison ; for this reason we must carefully watch all those to whom we administer this drug, if they

L

have not taken it before. In short, far from exerting a favourable action, and effecting the cure of secondary affections, Mercury may disturb the general health, and aggravate the manifestations of the disease in proportion to the quantity in which it is given. Under these circumstances the use of it must be suspended for a time, or until the patient shows an improvement in his general state of health, when recourse may be had to the remedy, and this time with more satisfactory results. In like manner, Mercury ought not to be continued when, after the period necessary for its action, it does not manifest any therapeutic effect. A suitable hygiene, combined with tonics, then becomes useful, as also the employment of certain mineral waters, and the water cure.

Such are the views and leading therapeutic agents employed by the highest allopathic authorities for the treatment of secondary symptoms, good in their way, but their arsenal contains too limited a number of weapons to meet the varied manifestations of this stage of the disease.

Let us therefore see what homœopathy can do.

"For the treatment of the various *syphilidæ*," writes the veteran Jahr, "we scarcely require any other remedies than those which are used for primary products (viz., chancre, buboes, mucous tubercles, and fig-warts), such as the various mercurial preparations, *Nitric Acid*, and *Thuja;* to which may be added *Aurum, Lycopodium, Staphysagria, Kali iodatum, Lachesis,* and in some cases *Hepar sulph.*, *Sarsaparilla,* and *Sulphur.*" This has been amply verified by Attomyr, Vehsemeyer, Lobethal, Clotter, Müller, Trink, and others, as well as by myself. In so far as mercury is concerned both schools are agreed, and by common consent give preference to the various compounds of that mineral, which in a large number of cases will effect all that is required. But there are other cases, which, from some peculiar idiosyncrasy of constitution, or from some antagonistic and resisting force in the system, will not yield kindly to any of the mercurial preparations, particularly when administered in the form of the crude drug, and even in the *first* or *second* decimal trituration ; but if first administered in the twelfth, and gradually descending to the lower potencies very satisfactory results frequently follow. This has occurred to me on several occasions. Failing this, we may then resort to *Nitric Acid, Phosphoric Acid, Lycopod.,* and *Aurum.* Jahr generally commences the treatment of secondaries with *Merc. sol.* or *Merc. præcip. rub.,* with an occasional change to *Merc. corr., Merc. nitros.* or *Cinnabaris,* and continues the use of the selected remedy for some time, unless no improvement follows in ten days or a fortnight ; or, the improvement obtained, ceases to continue. This is the mode of practice I am in the habit of adopting, and when I find the medicine loses its effects, or that the disease becomes stationary, I omit the selected drug for a few days, and give *Sulphur,* and recommence the mercurial preparation again.

For the early manifestations of those secondary phenomena, when they appear more or less conjointly with the primary lesion — the chancre—mercury stands foremost as our chief remedy, judiciously

chosen from the following list of preparations, viz.,
*Merc. vir., Merc. sol. Hah., Merc. sulph. rub., Merc.
præcip. rub., Merc. præcip. alb., Merc. chlorid., Merc.
bichlorid., Merc. nitros., Merc. biniodide,* and the
Merc. proto-iodide. The chief indications for the
selection of these mineral agents, conjointly with some
of the most approved anti-syphilitic vegetable
preparations, will be found in the following
arrangement.

1. For the *erythema roseola, papules, pustules,
vesicles, squamous* and *pigmentary* eruptions, with
or without the primary lesion, *Merc. sol. Hah.,
Merc. proto-iodide,* or the *Merc. biniodide* in the
first, second, or third decimal trituration, one grain
three times a day, which should be steadily persisted
in until the eruptions entirely disappear; "and when
a chancre appears at the same time," until that
product entirely heals and all callosity vanishes.

2. For angina syphilitica, which we sometimes,
encounter as the result of wet or cold, we shall not be
far wrong in commencing the treatment with a dose
or two of *Aconite* to subdue febrile symptoms, followed by *Apis, Bell.,* and the *Merc. sol.* or *Merc. corros.*

3. For those herpetic eruptions which sometimes
stud the mouth and throat, we have in *Lycopodium*
and *Nitric acid* admirable auxiliaries, fully confirmed by the experience of Hartmann and Jahr.

4. For excoriations and erosions in the mouth and
fauces, *Merc. sol., Nitric ac.,* and *Lachesis* will give
us material help.

5. For those elongated and patchy ulcers and
cracks which generally appear on the sides of the

tongue, *Merc. præc. ruber* and *Nitric acid* are our chief remedies. Many surgeons touch these ulcers with caustic.

6. For ulcers in the throat some of the mercurial preparations should first be selected, such as *Merc. sol. H. præc. ruber*, or *Bichlorid.*, followed by *Lachesis, Aurum Met., Lycopod., Iodine* (by inhalation), and the *Hydriodate of potass.*

7. For affections of the Schneiderian membrane, which at times becomes red and turgid, secreting a scanty, thick, yellowish matter, with loss of smell, *Merc. sol., Aur. met., Merc. biniod., Kali iodatum,* and *Bichromate of potass* are our chief remedies.

8. The testicles, or "more generally the epididymes," like the muscles and bones, undergo the influence of secondary syphilis. They sometimes accompany or closely follow the skin eruptions ; at other times they appear at a more remote period. Here also the mercurial preparations, such as the *proto* and *bin-iodide*, and gold, should be our chief medicines.

9. For bone pains, *ostitis*, and *periostitis* great relief will follow the administration of *Aconite, Mezereum,* or *Guaiacum,* and the local application of the tincture of aconite in the matrix form.

10. Syphilitic Ophthalmia. — Of all the manifestations of syphilis, writes Lancereux, the affections of the eyes are perhaps those which it is the most difficult to classify. They sometimes accompany the exanthematous syphilides ; sometimes, when more tardy in their appearance, they constitute, so to speak, a transition period between *secondary*

and *tertiary* affections. In general they invade the eye from its anterior to its posterior boundary, and are the more circumscribed and more serious, in proportion as the period at which they supervene is further removed from the first appearance of the primary lesion. In reality, no membranous structure of the eye is exempt from the attacks of syphilis ; the iris and choroid being the most liable. Mercury here also, the bichloride by preference, is our chief remedy. The first or second decimal trituration should be selected, one grain every second or third hour, either alone or in alternation with Bell., and a dose of Aconite every night. Irrespective of the anti-syphilitic properties of Mercury, that drug exercises a marked influence over all serous effusions ; and it is in this disease that Mercury most conspicuously displays its remedial powers, in preventing the deposition, and promoting the absorption of lymph ; it should be early administered, and continued during a period of some weeks.

11. For the sycosic excrescences which attend secondary symptoms, *Merc. sol.* and *Staphysagria,* with a solution of *Alum* or *Ant. tart.* as local applications, generally suffice in the majority of such cases.

TREATMENT OF THE TERTIARY AND QUATERNARY AFFECTIONS, otherwise known as Gummy Products.—" While the secondary manifestations of syphilis," writes Lancereux, " rarely require any other than a general treatment, the tertiary lesions, more deeply seated and more persistent, generally require further the employment of a local treatment, the hand of the surgeon being frequently required." IODINE is here the basis of our treatment, as was MERCURY in secondary syphilis. First administered by Martin and Lugol, it has more recently been lauded by Guillemin, who prescribes it according to the following formula:—Tincture of iodine, 5 parts; distilled water, 1,000 parts : two or three spoonfuls before each of the two chief meals of the day suffice in general, according to that author, to combat not only tertiary, but even secondary affections.

Iodine, however, is seldom given uncombined; recourse is most generally had to one of its salts, the iodide of potassium and Iodium. The dose in which iodide of potassium is given varies from seven and a half and fifteen grains to forty-five, sixty, seventy-five, and even ninety grains in twenty-four hours. Sŏme practitioners carry the dose to 150, 180, and 225 grains, or even more, but without advantage to the patients, for with iodide of potassium, as with all other medicinal agents, the organism cannot utilize more than a given quantity. Moreover, experience has shown that, under these circumstances, the therapeutic influence of the remedy is never in proportion to the dose taken, and that the pathogenetic effects alone are increased. The object of the physician in such cases is, therefore, to arrive gradually at a dose which produces therapeutic effects without producing pathogenetic effects injurious to the patient. This salt is administered in solution or in the syrup of gentian, saponaria, quassia, or sarsaparilla. Ricord gives it in syrup of gentian, 30 parts of potass to 500 of syrup, three table-spoonfuls daily; Melchior Robert in sarsaparilla. The larger

doses of iodide of potassium are generally given in
advanced and deep-seated lesions, such as diseases of
the bones and visceral localizations.   But if the
disease does not extend beyond the external or internal integument, and especially if the patient finds
himself in that stage of the complaint recognised by
some authors as the period of transition, the mixed
treatment as prescribed by Gibert and Bazin is the
best means of removing these symptoms, viz., the biniodide of mercury, combined with iodide of potassium ;
or syrup of the iodurated biniodide of mercury is the
preparation to be employed with most advantage
against deep-seated, tuberculo-ulcerated, and puro-
vesicular syphilides, affections for the most part
exceedingly obstinate.

Like mercury, the iodide of potassium destroys the
manifestation, but does not prevent relapses, and
consequently does not affect the diathesis.   The space
of time which it is desirable to continue the use of
this medicine is from two, three to four months, de-
pending of course on the obstinacy or otherwise of the
disease.   The iodide of iron in pills, or better still in
syrup, may be substituted with advantage, in debilitated persons, for the iodide of potassium, like the
mercurial preparations, and the preparations of iodine
require to be assisted in their action, whenever the
patient presents a certain degree of cachexia or anæmia.
Bitter drinks, infusion of cinchona, Bordeaux wine,
the juice of meat, roast meats, and even preparations
of iron become under these circumstances more or
less necessary.   Such are the views, and such is a
brief outline of the treatment adopted by the most

eminent of our allopathic brethren in the tertiary and visceral manifestations of syphilis.

Can homœopàthy do more? let us see. We will, however, *in limine* observe that the tertiary manifestations of supplies differ in many respects from the secondary phenomena; viz., they no longer retain their infecting properties; they are no longer transmissible to the fœtus; they seldom appear earlier than six months after the appearance of the primary lesion. This is, however, the shortest period. Cases have occurred where the disease has broken out ten, fifteen, or even twenty years after the first infection, either as local diseases or as general cachexia, and having lost all traces of a specific character, they degenerate into a form of dyscrasia analogous to scrofulosis, affect the whole organism, and develop what Astruc has truly said, " a world of diseases."

1. For the various exanthematous eruptions and gummy tumours which appear in the subcutaneous cellular tissues we shall not be far wrong in adopting the precepts laid down by our allopathic colleagues, by commencing the treatment with iodine and its compounds: failing this we may then resort to *Merc. sol.*, the biniodide and corrosive sublimate; and for pustular and scaly eruptions *Arsenicum,*which may be given in alternation with one of the mercurial preparations.

2. For alopecia, gummy tumours, ulceration of the scalp, and necrosis of the bony structure, we should commence with the *Iodide of potassium* or the *Biniodide of mercury*, followed by *Aur. met., Phosphorus* and *Mezereum.*

3. For gummy deposits in the mammary glands, *Merc. biniod.* and *Hydriodate of potash.*

For affections of the periosteum and bones, viz., bone pains, *Merc. sol., Merc. corr., Merc. biniodide,* and *Ars.;* periostitis, *Acon.* and *Mez.;* gummy tumours, *Merc. biniodide* and *Hydriodate of potassium;* exostosis, *Aur. m. mez.* and *Hydr. pot.;* caries, *Merc. corr.* and the *iodides.*

Caries of the facial bones, nasal and palatine, *Aur. m.* and *Mez.* ; caries of the humerus, jaw-bone, malar, tibia, and vertebræ, *Aur. m., Hep. s., Calc. c.* and *Sil.*

For affections of the testes, we have in the mercurial preparations *Aur. met., Con. clem., Iod., Pot., Puls., Phosph.* and *Sulph.,* admirable remedies, selected with due regard to all the concomitant symptoms.

For those deep perforating and serpiginous ulcers which attack the tongue, the soft parts of the mouth, the pharynx and larynx, likewise the skin, *Merc. corr., Iodine,* and its salts, constitute the chief remedies; and when these ulcers assume an indolent, ill-conditioned form, indisposed to heal, they should be touched once or twice a day with glycerine, alcohol, or tincture of iodine, or a weak solution of tincture of iodine, containing a small quantity of iodide of potassium. Some recommend touching these sores, particularly when they assume the serpiginous form, with nitrate of silver or perchloride of iron.

For the various visceral lesions, when we more particularly suspect gummy deposits, the treatment should be commenced with some of the mercurial preparations, followed by iodide of potassium, and

when considerable cachexia exists, leading us to suspect some amyloid degeneration of viscera, such as
the liver or spleen, " organs more frequently affected
with syphilis than any of the others," *Nitric acid* is
our chief remedy. Administered for a certain time
the acid possesses a remarkable tendency to cause
absorption of the morbid deposit to which the enlargement of the organs is due, to restore their normal
texture, and to produce an improvement of their
general conditions. For syphilitic affections of the
brain and spinal marrow, some of the mercurial preparations, *Iodide of Potassium,* and *Iron* are the
remedies we can place most confidence in.

PART VIII.

AUXILIARIES.

THE therapeutic and hygienic means which I am
in the habit of using as "helpmates" to the various
medicinal agents prescribed in this work, consist of
the turkish bath, hydropathy, or the water cure,
mineral waters, and diet.

TURKISH BATHS.—From the most civilized to the
most degraded of nations, sweating baths have been held
in high esteem as a curative agent. *Synonymously*, the
hammam of the Turks, the sudatorium of the Romans,
the temazcalli of the ancient Mexicans, the Abâyah
of the Arabs, and the Turkish bath of the English.
In the early treatment of the great syphilitic outbreak of the fourteenth century it was frequently used
by the leading syphilographers of that period. "In
difficult cases," writes Astruc, "they use bagnios, in
which the patients were thrown into a plentiful sweat,
by receiving the mild vapour of warm water, or the
smoke of perfumes, and thus the filth which adhered
to the skin was carried off." For poor people, instead
of bagnios, they promoted sweat by the heat of an
oven, and if we may believe Gaspar Torella, with
good success, for in his treatise *De Dolore in Puden
dagra*, 1500, he says, "that among all things which
he had tried for curing the *pains*, and even the *pustules*,
the best was to make the patient sweat in a hot oven

or bagnio for five days successively in the morning fasting."

The Turkish bath invariably renders me infinite service in the treatment of syphilis, in cases varying from the primary lesion to the tertiary and quaternary periods.

HYDROPATHY, or the so-called water cure, is another valuable adjuvant, and is very useful for combating the chloral anæmia so frequently met with in patients affected with constitutional syphilis : this influence is very marked in feeble lymphatic individuals with a tendency to scrofula. In fact, the good effects of the water treatment in the tertiary and quaternary stages cannot be denied ; and it is to be regretted that this mode of treatment is not more frequently applied, in lieu of the ponderous doses of the various mercurial and iodine compounds so freely prescribed by the majority of medical men. This treatment consists in a series of packing, douche, and sitz baths, in conjunction with the spirit lamp or Turkish bath.

MINERAL WATERS.—Jerome Fracastorius, in 1530, was about the first physician who drew the attention of the faculty to the value of mineral waters, particularly SULPHUR, as a curative agent in syphilitic diseases. The early syphilographers, however, regarded them as injurious, on account, most probably, of the property which they possess of developing manifestations which had previously remained latent. Thermal waters do not constitute a specific treatment for syphilis, but like the Turkish bath and the water cure, they render in the first place the system more susceptible to the action of medicines, and secondly, exert upon the most obstinate secondary and tertiary affections an action favourable to the employment of a specific treatment. Thus, under certain circumstances, especially in obstinate cases, conjoined with a low cachectic condition of the system, mineral waters are specially indicated, as they permeate the whole system, and give to the albumino-hydrargyrous compounds arrested in the web of the organs the fluidity necessary for the completion of the cure. Dassier, Pégot, and others, record some very interesting cases, which place beyond doubt the good effects of mineral waters when combined with the compounds of mercury and iodine. "Not only," says Pégot, "the thermal treatment combats successfully syphilitic affections, by imparting to mercury and iodine properties they no longer possessed, but it also stimulates the organism, restores languishing functions, especially of nutrition, and is one of the chief remedies to be opposed to syphilitic cachexia." Moreover it is not only sulphur waters which would appear to have the property of unmasking the hidden effects of syphilis; as the waters of Plombières, Vichy, and Carlsbad, have in many intances brought to light old syphilitic affections.

Warm sulphur waters take precedence, however, of all the other classes of mineral waters when it is a question of assisting the cure of syphilis or of reproducing its manifestations. Of these we may mention the thermal springs of Bath, Hotwells, Clifton, Matlock, Buxton, and Knaresborough; and the cold sulphur of Nottingham and Radipole at Weymouth, Giesland in Cumberland, Holbeck near Leeds,

Askern near Doncáster, Harrogate in Yorkshire, the
famous waters of Llandegly and Llan-y-drindod in
Radnorshire, and the bromo-iodine water of the
Woodhall Spa, Lincolnshire.

On the continent the thermal waters of Barèges
Aix-la-Chapelle, Weilbach, and Kreuznach, whenever the syphilis is accompanied by scrofulosis, in
which case it is generally obstinate.

DIETETICS.

Diet has from the earliest times been regarded as
a powerful auxiliary in the treatment of syphilis ;
and the ancient syphilographers attached far more
importance to it than those of the present time.
They strictly adhered to the ninth aphorism of
Hippocrates, which signifies, " the more impure bodies
are nourished, the worse they grow." They gave
meats of easy digestion, and such other things as
might tend to cleanse the blood. According to Fracastor a syphilitic patient was forbidden to. leave his
bed for a whole month, was only allowed just sufficient nourishment to sustain life, viz., three or four
ounces of bread, two ounces of chicken, and one ounce
of raisins. He was debarred from taking wine or
any other stimulant, and took as his only drink a
weak decoction of guaiacum sweetened with honey.
Afterwards he recommended exercise in the open
air, the pure air of the hills, the pleasures of the
chase, the tillage of the land, the exercise of wrest-
ling, leaping, tennis, and riding. Fallopius in 1560,
and Brassavolus in 1553, wrote in the same strain,
and the latter gives a striking instance of the good

effects of gymnastics in the history of a man who cured himself of nocturnal pains by going often to pull the rope of the great bell of Ferrara. In like manner it is by diet that the inhabitants of Abyssinia, the fellahs of Egypt, the negroes of Africa, and other half-civilized and barbarous nations cure their venereal affections-

It follows from this "that rules and indications exist in dietetics." The food should be little changed, for the habits of the patient should be respected. As a general rule the diet should be plain, simple, and nourishing, cocoa, milk, or tea, with a moderate amount of bread and butter, or stewed fruit, for breakfast. Roast or boiled (fresh) meat, with a fair quantity of seasonable vegetables for dinner ; and if the patient be accustomed to stimulants he may be allowed a moderate quantity of some light wine, such as a red or white Burgundy or Bordeaux, or the Hungarian, Edenbergh, or Somlau. The evening meal should consist of either plain black tea, cocoa, or porridge, with an ordinary amount of bread and butter, or stewed fruit. The amount and quality of the food must, however, be selected in accordance with the general constitution of the patient ; for a low diet, if injudiciously prescribed, will sometimes aggravate the disease, while a reparative and tonic one will constitute the condition of a successful treatment. Pure fresh air also should not be neglected. "Remember," writes Diday, "that the *air* and *sun* bath often becomes a succour which is indispensable for those subjects in whom vital action languishes. Inaction, both of body and mind, is at all times a serious

obstacle to a rapid and satisfactory cure of syphilis ;
and without requiring so much as Fracastor did, a
patient so afflicted should continue to attend to his
usual occupation, and during his leisure hours he
should undertake pleasant walks, fencing, riding,
gymnastics, join in agreeable society, read some light
amusing works, or any other occupation that would
tend to divert the mind from pondering over the
subtle poison still lurking in the system. Continence
is another hygienic measure which should be strictly
observed by a patient so afflicted ; he should avoid
the pleasures of the flesh as well as the pleasures of
the table, and enjoy with the greatest moderation
women as well as wine. High living, spirituous
liquors, and tobacco should be strictly prohibited ;
they are a source of infinite mischief, and have but
too often occasioned symptoms which otherwise
perhaps would never have manifested themselves ; and
they so change the character of a disease as to convert
a mild form into a malignant one, in illustration of
which many cases are recorded in other sections of
this work.

M

PART IX.

ONANISM.

IT would be foreign to the scope of this work to depict the effects of this unnatural vice on those who are the victims of it during childhood. Suffice it to say, careful watching, moral tonics, and the careful selection of the indicated remedy to be hereafter mentioned, will eradicate the evils resulting from the pernicious practice. When perpetrated by those of adult age, however, its symptoms and treatment will differ in the male and female sexes; hence it will be convenient to divide our subject under the two heads of (1) male onanism, and (2) female onanism.

1. MALE ONANISM.—This is usually accomplished by friction of the virile member by the hand in the early stages; and it may be defined as *seminal emission obtained by other means than that of sexual intercourse*, for it will be found that before long this emission will take place without even the slightest friction. When first practised the whole sensual orgasm is in an excited condition. The penis is frequently erect, the passions fervid, and the gratification intense. The ejaculation follows prolonged irritation of the penis only, being but seldom nocturnal. This stage of excitement is soon succeeded by *corresponding* depression—a depression, both moral,

sexual, and physical. The symptoms are those which affect the system—constitutionally; and those which affect the irritated part—locally.

Constitutional Effects.—These are mental debility, corporeal lassitude, sunken eye, dilated pupil, pale face, emaciated frame, and nervous prostration; society is shunned, and all exertion avoided.

Local Effects.—The emission now takes place involuntarily, or is occasioned by a lewd thought or a lascivious glance, and becomes *nocturnal.* Erection is feeble, and at times absent; the semen runs from the flaccid penis as it chafes against the trousers whilst walking, or even whilst the victim of the debasing vice is passing water or fæces. All voluptuous feeling is gone long before the patient ceases to masturbate. If continued till this stage arrives, epilepsy or insanity closes the scene—"he ceases to be a man." The constitution is undermined, the system enervated, the intellect weakened, and he sinks into a grave dug by his own folly, and filled by a body polluted by his evil practices.

2. FEMALE ONANISM.—This is far more frequently practised than some would try to persuade us, whilst it acts in an equally injurious manner upon the constitution. The local symptoms are those of an elongated, highly irritable, or often hypertrophied clitoris, and a subacute inflammation of the vagina, giving rise to a slight discharge of acrid greenish leucorrhœal matter· There is also considerable irritability of the bladder.

TREATMENT.—1st, and of vital importance, is the avoidance of the cause ; 2nd, frequent ablution of the loins and private parts with cold water ; 3rd, regulation of the hygienic surroundings—by use of simple diet, abstinence from stimulants, plenty of exercise in the open air, early hours, large airy bedroom, and hard mattress (not lying on back) ; 4th, the substitution of healthy moral literature for the prurient trash which so constantly forms the library of the youth of the present day ; 5th, dissipation is to be shunned, and slight intellectual occupation sought ; and 6th, to administer one of the following remedies, great care being taken in its selection.

Veratrum Viride, in the early stages, and before the habit is formed ; when emissions take place frequently, and after study, cheerful company, or more than once in the week. It may be given in $\frac{1}{2}$ or $\frac{1}{4}$ drop doses of the third dilution every four hours.

Calc. Carb. is one of the most frequently useful medicines ; it is indicated for great pain in the back of the head and neck, and between the shoulders, after emission, with great depression of spirits and mental confusion, and loss of memory. The habit is fully formed, but a great desire is felt to be freed from it. The prescription should be—Calc. Carb. 3x three times a day, and Sulph. 30, twice a week.

Phos. Acid cures the debility of onanists ; it also removes absence of sexual desire, the profuse perspirations, frequent erections without desire for coitus, discharge of semen during a stool or while urinating, and a gnawing pain in the testicles. Third dilution is the best.

Staphysagria is indicated by excitement of the sexual instinct, followed by hypochondriacal indifference. After emission there is great weakness of the arms, the eyes are sleepy and surrounded by a dark ring ; weakness of memory and dullness of the intellect, with inability to perform any mental labour; dislike to society and conversation. The 3x dilution is the most serviceable, and should be followed by Calc. Carb. China is required when there is desire to be alone, great anxiety and discouragement, general debility, emaciation, nocturnal emissions which cause excessive weakness in the morning, drawing pains in the testicles, sexual desire is excited with lascivious fancies. Third dilution bis die.

Carbo Veget. is a most useful medicine in female onanists ; there is present a greenish corrosive discharge from the vagina ; itching, burning, soreness of the vulva, and disposition to miscarriages ; also great excitability of the sexual system, and great weakness on making the least exertion. The sixth dilution is the best.

China or Merc. Sol. is often useful after Carbo Veget. There is lascivious excitement with painful nightly erections, nightly emissions of semen mixed with blood. The penis is small, cold, and flabby ; dragging pain in the testes and spermatic cord ; emission is soon followed by icy cold hands, burning or bruised pain in the back, with sensation of weakness. Merc. Sol. 6.

Cantharis : satyriasis ; frequent and ready pollutions ; emission is followed by burning pain in the urethra, with violent nocturnal priapism.

Sepia : in discharge of semen during a difficult evacuation or after urinating. In females, with yellowish or green leucorrhœa, bearing down in the

uterus, with induration of the neck of the womb ;
shootings in the vagina with excoriation.

*Of the Names bestowed at Various Times upon
Syphilis.*—As various as have been the opinions of
physicians on the nature of the disease, so proportionately various have been the designations bestowed
upon it.   Regarding it as many have done, as a form
of *lepra* derived from Asia, it became known as
Elephantiasis.   Others saw in it a cutaneous disorder
known among the Arabs as *sahafati.*   But the familiar
name bestowed upon it by the first physicians, after
its enormous spread, was derived from its remarkable
similarity to the small-pox.   The following list gives
a fair outline of the various names thus employed to
indicate it : —

Country or Nation.	Common Name.	Name produced by National Rancour.	Name produced by Religious Impulses.
Africans	Pian. Yaws. Frambœsia.	—	—
American aborigines ...	Galel-ya.	Tepea.	—
Arabians	Sahafati.	—	—
Aragonians... ...	Las bubas.	—	Mal de St. Sementus.
Calcutta	Pockas Wallahs.	—	—
Catalonians ...	Las bubas.	—	Mal de St. Sementus.
Chinese	Konang Tong Tchouang.	Mal Portuguese.	—
Dutch	Spanse Poken.	—	—
English	Syphilis.	French Pox.	Foul disorder.
Flemish	Les Poques.	Spanish Pox.	Spaanse Pocken.
French	Grose Vairole.	Mal de Naples.	Mal de St. Roche.
Genoese	Lo male de le tavelle.	Mal de Frances.	Mal de St. Job.
Germans	Grosse Blätter.	Franzosen.	FranzösischePocken.
Indians, East ...	—	Mal de Portugais.	—
Indians, West ...	Pian. Yaws. Frambœsia.	—	—
Italians	Mal Fránces.	Mal de Frantzos.	Mal de St. Job.
Japanese	—	Fire of lust.	—

Country or Nation.	Common Name.	Name produced by National Rancour.	Name produced by Religious Impulses.
Latins	Lues Venerea.	Morbo Gallico.	—
Lombards	Lo male delle Bozzole.	—	Mal de St. Job.
Moors	—	Mal de Espagnol	—
Neapolitans	—	Mal Franks.	Mal de St. Job.
Persians	—	Mal de Turcos.	—
Picardians	Les poques.	.	Mal de St. Job.
Poles	—	Mal de Allemand.	—
Portuguese	Ospa, or Vospa.	Mal de Castillan.	—
Russians	—	Mal de Polonais.	—
St. Domingo	Guaguara hipas, taybat, ycas.	—	Mal de St. Job.
Savoyards	Clavlée.	—	—
Scotch	Sibbens, or Sewens.	—	—
Spaniards	Las Bubas, or Boas.	—	—
Swedes	Radesy-ge.	—	—
Turks	—	Mal des Franks.	—
Welsh	Y frech losg.	Yr hen Gl.	Y Clefyd drwg.

PART X.

COMMENTS ON THE CONTAGIOUS DISEASES ACTS.

AMONG all the diseases that weigh upon suffering humanity, there are probably none which are more extensively discussed by physicians, more dreaded by some, more frivolously treated by others, and at the same time less definitely determined, with regard to their course, the multifarious phenomena they assume, and the boundaries of their various forms and destructive inroads upon the framework and constitution of both sexes, than the motley group of diseases designated as VENEREAL. According to the views of Nicholaus Leonicenus and Gaspar Torella in the fourteenth century; James Cataneus, John Almener, Peter Maynard, Jerome Fracastorius, Nicholas Massa, John de Vigo, and Paracelsus in the fifteenth century; Hartmann and others in the sixteenth century; Petronius Cæsalpinus, the supposed discoverer of the circulation of the blood, John Deraux, Fallopius, Girtanner, Astruc, John Hunter, and others in the seventeenth century—among the older authorities: or Carmichael, Bell, Cazenove, Biett, Lancereux, Diday, Ricord, Hutchinson, and many more among recent physicians; there exists nothing more disgusting, revolting, and insidious in the whole world than these diseases. Fostered as they undoubtedly are, in the fatal bosom of a degrading passion, and conceived at a moment of burning and illicit lust, they scatter, according to some silently and mysteriously, their poisonous seed, whose offspring, which at its first appearance is but slightly regarded, and extirpated from the sphere of observation as speedily as possible by the criminal hand of indiscreet or ignorant practitioners ; nevertheless continues silently to unfold its manifold germs in the organism, until they break forth anew in a variety of different forms, and thus announce to every eye the presence of the still raging malady. Again and again repressed by external means, and again sprouting forth in other parts of the body, they penetrate, according to the assertions of recent observers, all the tissues of the sufferer, who, far from suspecting the hydra-headed monster that is gnawing at his vital forces, but too often sees one organ after the other invaded, tortured, and destroyed ; his face disfigured in the most horrible manner ; his muscles and bones perforated ; his mind converted into a moping idiot, or a madman gay ; his nerves palsied ; his eyesight lost or bedimmed, and his once healthy frame overwhelmed by the most horrid and excruciating tortures, without knowing how his distress can be alleviated, were it only in the most trifling degree.

Whatever revolting and horrifying diseases are met with in large towns, in the huts of misery, and in the gloomy abodes of vice ; all those miserable-looking wretches who are covered with ugly scars and jagged ulcers ; whose faces are disfigured by pustules and suppurating blotches ; who are not unfrequently deprived of their noses, their sight, their hearing, their smell, and their power of swallowing ; who are emaciated to skeletons; whose livid, pustulous, and shrivelled skin is dangling upon their fleshless bones like some pestiferous shroud ; and who, spreading a pestilential fœtor all around, wander about like half-rotten spectres from the gloomy recesses of the tombs; or who, removed from all human society, and avoided even by their own friends, are stretched upon the torture-bed of hopeless despair, praying for death as their greatest blessing : all these unfortunate and miserable-looking objects, according to the opinion of the greatest physicians of this and past centuries, owe the whole sum of their sufferings to no other cause than to syphilitic infection ; which, having been contracted in an unguarded moment, had been neglected, disregarded, and afterwards but too often mismanaged and badly treated throughout.   Yet the science of pathology has up to the present time made such wonderful advances, that a whole army of the most chronic, incurable, and deep-seated organic affections, which assume a thousand colours, and the most hideous and fantastic garbs, with which inhabitants of large cities and towns, the soldiers of our armies and the sailors of our fleets, and the youth of our country are afflicted ; emanates from this single CAUSE as their true fountain-head ; their true character, unless they had reached the previously described fearful height, being almost always misapprehended, so that they are confounded with other and less dangerous diseases, and the virus, even if, favoured by peculiar

circumstances, it should not break forth in actual
disease in all cases, is transmitted to the offspring,
and entails upon them the distressing and irresistible
processes of destruction from which the guilty parents
had luckily escaped, thus confirming the sacred
and solemn warning, that "the sins of the fathers"
are visited "on the children to the third and
fourth generation." It is the opinion of the more
advanced syphilographers of the present day, that
these diseases contain a poison which, if once introduced into the system, germinates and sprouts after
the fashion of parasitical growths, at the expense of
its vital essence and strength, and continues to spread
and sprout until the body perishes by the poison.
And when nothing is done against these diseases
than merely to obliterate their sprouting growths by
outward applications, the roots remain in the organic
tissues, and may sprout forth again and again until
life is annihilated by this murderous destroyer.

The frightful prevalence and virulence of this
disease among the lower class of prostitutes in certain
seaports, garrison towns, and in the neighbourhood of
camps, had for many years attracted the serious attention of the Legislature; and in 1862 a special
committee was appointed by the Government to
inquire into the prevalence of "venereal diseases" in
the army and navy. . Their report, dated the 15th
December, contains, at its conclusion, the following :—

"Your committee have refrained from entering
into the painful details which have come to their
knowledge of the state of our naval and military
stations at home as regards prostitution.

"These facts are so appalling that they feel it a duty to press on the Government the necessity of at once grappling with the mass of vice, filth, and disease which surrounds the soldiers' barracks and the seamen's homes, which not only crowds our hospitals with the sick, weakens the roll of our EFFECTIVES, and swells the list of our invalids, but which surely, however slowly, saps the vigour of our soldiers and our seamen, sows the seeds of degradation and degeneracy, and causes an amount of suffering difficult to over-estimate."

The reports of Government committees are not, as a rule, of a sensational description, more generally they are dry and technical documents. Very terrible, then, must have been the condition of matters, when a Government committee concluded their report in such terms as these. It, however, two years afterwards (1864) resulted in the passing of an Act for the prevention of contagious diseases at certain naval and military stations; namely, Portsmouth, Plymouth, and Devonport.

In the same year, a committee, consisting of some of the most eminent physicians and surgeons in London, was appointed by the Admiralty to inquire into the pathology and treatment of syphilis and syphiloidal diseases, and to suggest practical rules for the prevention of those diseases, capable of being adopted by the naval and military authorities. Such inquiry lasted over a period of nearly two years; and the result of this inquiry was that a mass of facts and practical experience was accumulated, in reference to the pathology and treatment, both hygienically

and medically, such as had never before been collected
to elucidate the nature of any one disease.   The
attention of the committee had been especially drawn
to the laws which had been enforced in Malta, in
which island the regular periodical examination of
all known prostitutes, and the detention in hospital of
any who were found diseased, had resulted in the total
extinction of venereal disease so far as the island was
concerned, all fresh cases being clearly traced to
fresh importation.

In 1866, a fresh Act was framed, entitled " An Act
for the better Prevention of Contagious Diseases at
certain Naval and Military Stations." This repealed
the Act of 1864, and with some alterations is now in
force.   The benefits derived from the working of this
Act were so satisfactory, physically, morally, and
socially in the districts where it was extended,
that an association was formed in London, consisting
of some of the leading members of the medical, clerical,
and legal professions, university professors, eminent
statesmen and philanthropists, with the view of
petitioning Parliament for an extension of the Act to
the civil population of our large towns.   In consequence of the importance of this movement, a
committee of the House of Lords was in 1868
appointed to consider the subject.   Their report contains the following recommendation:—" The committee consider the the cautious extension of the Act
may be safely entrusted to Government, and consequently recommend the introduction into Parliament
of a bill giving to her Majesty in Council power to apply
the Act of 1866 not only to all naval and military

stations, but also to any locality the inhabitants of which may apply to be included in the operations of the Act." The witnesses examined on that committee consisted of some of the leading medical men in London and other large towns. In 1869 a committee of the Commons was appointed to inquire into the working of the Act of 1866; and although the Act had only been in operation two years and a half, and at some stations only seven months, strong testimony was borne to the benefits, both in a moral and sanitary point of view, which had resulted from it.

Prostitution appears to have considerably diminished, its most aggravated features to have toned down, and its physical features considerably abated. It was further resolved that the Act should extend to other places, viz., Gravesend, Maidstone, Winchester, Dover, Deal, Walmer, Canterbury, Dartmouth, Ivybridge, and Southampton: great stress was laid by the committee, as to whether it would not be advisable and practicable to extend to the civil population the benefits of an Act which had in so short a time done so much to diminish prostitution, decrease disease, and reclaim so many women from an abandoned and debased life.

The Acts of 1864 and 1866 passed with very little opposition; but after the formation of the association for promoting the extension of the Acts, and the report of the committee of the House of Lords, a general "hue and cry" was raised, with a most determined opposition to the further expansion of these Acts.

In 1870 the first motion for the repeal of the Acts

was brought before the House of Commons, the debate being held with closed doors. The motion, as it should be, was negatived by a large majority.

I have given these few details in order that a clear insight may be obtained as to why these Acts of Parliament were ever passed, and, having passed, why they were continued.

The Act of 1866 was passed in accordance with the recommendations of the highest medical authorities, after a most laborious and painstaking inquiry, extending over a period of two years. Moreover, on the strength of such a report, both Houses of Parliament not only confirmed it, but strongly recommended its extension, which was partly adopted in the Act of 1869.

The different localities in which the Acts are now in force are—

In England: Aldershot, Canterbury, Chatham, Colchester, Dartmouth, Deal, Devonport, Dover, Folkestone, Gravesend, Maidstone, Portsmouth, Plymouth, Sheerness, Shorncliffe, Southampton, Walmer, Winchester, Windsor, and Woolwich.

In Ireland: Cork, the Curragh, and Queenstown.

From this it will be seen that the Acts at present applied only to some garrison towns and certain naval seaports ; the large seaport towns of Liverpool, Bristol, Hull, Swansea, Cardiff, Newport, Glasgow, Edinburgh, Dundee, and Belfast ; and our great seats of learning, Oxford and Cambridge, where the disease commits terrible havoc and disastrous results amongst the undergraduates, being conspicuous by

, their absence. It is most important that the list of places here quoted should be carefully studied and frequently referred to, as it is surprising how much ignorance there is even amongst people whom we should expect to find well informed on so grave a subject and foul a disease—a disease which has for ages been undermining and sapping to its very foundation the constitution of man, and disseminating its destructive and malignant seed to the second and third generation. It will help us to understand how, on the one hand, these' Acts are TOO partially applied to have any particular influence in reducing the frequency of the disease beyond the very limited boundaries to which they are at present applied; on the other hand, however, these districts are sufficiently numerous and expansive to enable us to judge of the marked good effects produced by the careful and proper, working of these Acts in a MEDICAL, MORAL, and SOCIAL point of view, as fully confirmed by personal inquiries and Governmental reports.

The Royal Commissioners, to whom this painful and delicate subject was entrusted, were the Right Hon. W. N. Massey; the Right. Hon. Viscount Hardinge; the Right Rev. the Bishop of Carlisle; the Right Hon. Lord Hampton; the Right Hon. W. F. Cowper-Temple; Sir J. S. Trelawny, Bart.; Sir W. C. James, Bart.; Vice-Admiral Collinson; Charles Buxton, Esq.; Major O'Reilly, M.P.; Peter Rylands, Esq., M.P.; A. J. Mundella, Esq., M.P.; Professor Huxley; the Rev. Canon Gregory; the Rev. J. F. D. Maurice; the Rev. Dr. Hannah; Dr. Samuel Wilks; Dr. J. H. Bridges; Dr. G. E. Paget; T. Holmes, Esq.,

N

F.R.C.S. ; H. Coote, Esq. ; G. W. Hastings, Esq., and R. Applegarth, Esq.

It will thus be seen that the clergy, the bar, the medical profession, the army and the navy, were all fairly represented on the Commission, which, as will appear, comprised stern opponents of the Acts, supporters, and others who may be fairly considered as strictly neutral.

In December, 1870, the Commissioners sat to take evidence of the working of the Acts ; some eighty witnesses were examined, amongst whom were various official personages and officers of high rank in the public services ; inspectors of police forces, inspectors of certified hospitals, several surgeons engaged in the administration of the Acts, various others officially connected with different lock hospitals, refuges, and reformatories, besides many clergymen of various denominations.

A large amount of evidence was received on the subject of venereal disease, its classification, different forms, and diagnosis, and its effects on the constitution of the sufferers.

Substantially, the authorities were agreed that the disease is contagious ; that even in its milder form it frequently involves for a time painful and disabling complications, which leave permanent local and constitutional damage behind them ; and that many innocent persons, married and unmarried, including medical men and nurses, may and do often suffer from the contagion ; and further, that the posterity of a diseased parent are liable to serious affection from constitutional syphilis.

The voluminous statistics laid before the Commissioners, in the returns of the army and navy medical departments, and the metropolitan police returns, showing the number of brothels and public women, and of the proportions of disease in the protected districts, at various periods since the Act of 1864, received marked attention from them.

They go far to prove a marked improvement in the health of the army and navy under the new system.

They go to prove a marked reduction of the disease among the lower class of prostitutes, as well as improvement in their morals and mode of conducting themselves ; soldiers and sailors, under the influence of drink, being no longer importuned and seized upon by filthy and degraded prostitutes, as they were in former days. The Contagious Diseases Acts have in one sense acted as a SANITARY SCAVENGER, by purging the towns and encampments to which they have been applied of miserable creatures who were reeking masses of rottenness, and pestiferous vehicles of disease ; and moreover they have provided those unfortunate "outcasts of society" with asylums where their sufferings could be temporarily relieved, even if it were not within the pale of science to eradicate the rank poison from the system.

But the alleviation of the physical sufferings of these unfortunate and frail sisters is not the only good that has accrued to them from these Acts ; and although the reclamation of fallen women seems hardly to have entered into the original conception of the Acts, it very soon became recognised as a prominent section of the system. A chaplain is attached to each of the certified hospitals. The matrons are mostly of a superior class, qualified by long experience for the performance of their duties, and animated by a benevolent zeal for the work in which they are engaged ; and such is the influence which has been brought to bear upon the inmates, that many have returned to the bosom of their friends, others to homes and refuges always open and ready for their reception, and some have emigrated to other climes and are doing well.

The good moral effects which these Acts have already produced may be thus briefly stated :—

A.   Religious and sound moral influence has been brought to bear upon large numbers of women ; a large portion of whom had been from infancy familiar only with scenes of debauchery and vice.

B.   Many towns and camps have been cleared, or nearly so, of the miserable women who were formerly to be found in their streets and thoroughfares, their only places of rest at night being hedges and ditches, railway arches, bridges, and reeking sewers.

C.   A considerable number of these unfortunates have been reclaimed and restored to respectable life, and in many instances married.

D.   The number of loose women has been greatly reduced, and those who remain have been rendered more decent and decorous in appearance and conduct.

E.   The practice of clandestine prostitution, which too often degenerates into open professional vice, has been materially checked by fear of the consequences of such illicit indulgence which are rendered probable under the Acts.

F. The sad spectacle of juvenile prostitutes of tender age, so rife in localities heretofore, has been greatly diminished, and in some instances almost entirely removed.

G. The temptations by which young men of all classes have been hitherto assailed have been to a great extent taken out of their way, and a higher tone of morality has thus been promoted.

The Commissioners who drew up the report, concluded by saying: "We are of opinion that the total repeal of these Acts would be, as was said by a Devonport witness, 'disastrous in the extreme.' We object to attempting a compromise, which would probably be unsuccessful, by retreating on an imperfect measure discredited by grave and obvious faults, and we desire to see the Acts of 1866 and 1869 fully maintained in substance and in principle."

In 1871 a memorial, signed by two thousand five hundred of the leading members of the medical profession, was presented to Parliament in favour of the continuance of the Acts.

In 1870, 1873, and 1875, motions were moved in the House of Commons for the total repeal of these useful and benevolent Acts; an amendment was on each occasion proposed and carried by a large majority, that these Acts should not be repealed, which was fully confirmed by the House of Lords.

The Right Hon. Dr. Lyon Playfair, M.P. for the Universities of Edinburgh and St. Andrews in 1870, in a speech which was marked by profound learning and deep antiquarian research on the subject, referred to the rules and ordinances of eighteen houses of bad repute (stews) situate on the Bankside, Southwark, as far back as 1430, which were under the jurisdiction of the Bishop of Winchester. In the year 1497 the Aberdeen magistrates caused all women who were diseased to abandon their evil courses and shut themselves up in their houses till they were cured, branding on the cheek with a red-hot key those who came out too soon. Six months later the Privy Council ordered the authorities of Edinburgh to collect all diseased women, with their doctors, on the sands of Leith, boats being provided to transport them to the island of Inchkeith, where they were to remain till cured, on pain of being branded in a similar manner. In 1529, Parliament arraigned Cardinal Wolsey for daring to go into the presence of his sovereign while he was suffering from the foul disease, when he ought to have isolated himself from all in whom the State was interested.

This enforced isolation of DISEASED PERSONS we have now mentioned extends to those gallant men who are kept for the protection of the State both by sea and land; and it is fervently to be hoped that the time is not far distant when these beneficent Acts will throw their protective powers over the whole of England and her far-distant and extensive colonies ; for no one except those who have paid more than ordinary attention to venereal disease can for a moment conceive the frightful and loathsome ravages it inflicts upon the human body, or the appalling mortality from the same cause. Dr. Frederick W. Lowndes, of Liverpool, to whom I am indebted for a copy of a well - written

pamphlet on this subject, gives us some valuable
statistics relative to the ratio of mortality in Liverpool and other large towns from venereal diseases, also the extent of prostitution :—

Liverpool in 1871 had a population of 493,346
     ,,   ,,   brothels   668
     ,,   ,,   prostitutes   1,722

At the present time the number of these unfortunates
has increased in proportion to the increase of population.

Deaths from syphilis from 1860 to 1875, a period
of sixteen years, have been as follows :—

Males 900
Females 700
Infants under one year ... 2,016

It must not, however, be supposed that these are by
any means the total number of deaths from this terrible
disease, as many deaths doubtless have been set
down to other causes than syphilis, more particularly
in infants.

Dr. Lowndes, whose able treatise I have freely
drawn upon, being anxious to see something of the
practical working of the Acts, visited Aldershot,
Chatham, Plymouth, and Devonport in 1875. As
Plymouth resembles Liverpool in being a seaport and
a great maritime highway, Dr. Lowndes was specially
interested in seeing the stipulations of the Acts being
carried out. When the Act of 1864 was first put
into operation, in the following year, there were 356
brothels and 1,770 prostitutes in Plymouth and Devonport. The number of beds available for diseased

females in the Royal Albert Hospital at that time
was only 38, quite inadequate for the purpose. In

February, 1866, the number was increased to 50
April   „   „   „   62
January, 1868   „   „   86
February „   „   „   96
March   „   „   „   112
April   „   „   „   128
May   „   „   „   154
July   „   „   „   162

With this INCREASED accommodation the disease
proportionately DECREASED, and the character of the
disease became materially changed, becoming much
milder and more amenable to treatment. The reduction and diminished virulence of the disease, however,
is not by any means the only good which has been
effected in Plymouth and Devonport. The number
of prostitutes, as we have seen, at first 1,770, has
been since reduced to about 400 ; and the number of
brothels from 356 to 98. At one time it was impossible
to walk the streets without being solicited and insulted
by the lowest of women, whose language and de-
meanour were shocking. Now, crowds of drunken
seamen and shameless and abandoned women round
public-houses are never seen ; and even those streets
still inhabited by those unfortunates are quiet and
orderly. Chatham, Aldershot, Windsor, Dover, Canterbury, and Portsmouth, showed results equally as
satisfactory.

The following extract of a letter from Dr. Gram-
shaw, the visiting surgeon under the Acts, and medical

officer of health at Gravesend, which appeared in a recent number of the *British Medical Journal*, shows very clearly the excellent results in that town :—

" The tables of statistics put forward both by promoters and opponents of the Contagious Diseases Acts are frequently so bewildering to ordinary minds that they are cast aside without examination, and the statements of those who frame them are taken for granted, whatever may be the opinions they are wanted to produce.

" A statement of facts with regard to the working of the Acts amongst us in Gravesend, if unencumbered by tables, may perhaps be interesting to some, and may also be useful in the present unsettled state of public opinion.

" We have on the books here a number of women, varying from thirty-five to forty, somewhat under one-half of whom are required to come up weekly for inspection. This of course represents the number of public prostitutes only. The behaviour of these women has been uniformly good. There has never been the slightest repugnance shown by any to *examination.* During my two years of office I have known girls come into the district from Warley and elsewhere to present themselves for examination, but I never once heard or saw any unwillingness to submit to it on the score of modesty from a single patient. A few object to the trouble it gives them of getting clean clothes, and of regularity of hours, but *never* from any other cause. No officer has ever been found *overstepping* the limits of his duty. In the last four months I have been obliged to send only *one* woman to hospital for decided disease, and either three or four others as doubtful cases, whose detention has only been for a short period.

" In private practice here I rarely see a case of syphilis, either in men or women, *certainly not contracted in the town.* In conversation with other medical men I hear their experience is nearly the same. At all events, the amount in the last few years is very much lessened. The chemists, who used themselves to treat a great many venereal diseases, make a similar statement.

"Our barracks contain a variable number of soldiers; I believe the average number to be about 400. Since June 17, 1875, there have been in the Military Hospital no more than *three* cases of the disease, one only of these as ascribed to Gravesend ; the other two were contracted before the men came here. When we take this last statement into consideration, and recollect that, though not exactly a port, vessels are always passing and re-passing on the river, and that they are often detained here for a day or two, we may fairly give credit to the Acts, and to their REPRESSIVE and PROTECTIVE POWERS for much of this freedom from a foul and horrible scourge.

" To those who would accuse us, as they often do, of bringing up for examination women who are only suspected of prostitution, we reply that nothing of the sort ever takes place. It is necessary to be certain of their character before they are summoned to attend ; and though there are now and then cases where the suspicion is very strong, yet the Acts are never put in force against them till certainty exists. To such as

publicly commit themselves we say, we are power-
less to prevent you exercising your calling if you will
persist in doing so ; but we can, and will, to a certain
extent, prevent your becoming the source of irreparable mischief to infants and unoffending victims.
All this takes place quietly and decorously, in a secluded
part of every town where the Acts are in force ; and
if any part of the system can possibly be called
objectionable, it is well and fully counterbalanced by
ITS GOOD RESULTS."

REMEDIES.

THE remedies recommended by many authors, and referred to throughout the pages of this work, consist of a solution of Alum, Arnica montana, Calendula officinalis, Bichloride of mercury, Carbolic acid, Condy's fluid, Sulphate of zinc, Nitrate of silver, and Nitric acid.

The Carbo-sulphuric paste of Ricord.

The Chloride of zinc paste of Diday.

The Potassa fusa vel Potassa c. calce of Parker.

The Nitric acid of the author.

The Opiate cerate of Lancereux.

The internal remedies chiefly recommended by French physicians consist of Bazin's syrup, of the following proportions.—Take—

Biniodide of Mercury . . .	0·15 parts,
Iodide of Potassium	10·15 ,,
Syrup of Saponaria	500·00 ,,

Two tablespoonfuls are given daily at first, and after wards increased to four.

Belloste's pills.—Take—

Metallic Mercury . . . ⎱
Aloes . . . . ⎰ *aa* 0·75 grains,

Rhubarb . . . . . . } aa 0·30 grains,
Scammony . . . . . }
Black Pepper . . . . . . 0·15 „

Mix for one pill.

Sédillot's pills.—Take—
Strong Mercurial Ointment . 1·5 grains,
Medicinal Soap . . . } aa 1·5 „
Powdered Marsh Mallow }

For one pill.

Van Swieten's drops.—Take—
Bichloride of Mercury . . . 12 parts,
Corn Spirit . . . . . . 1,000 „

A tablespoonful to be taken morning and evening.

Mialhe's formula.—Take—
Bichloride of Mercury . . . 15 grains,
Chloro-hydrate of Ammonia . 75 „
The whites of two eggs
Distilled water . . . . . . 30 ounces.

From one to three tablespoonfuls to be taken daily.

Cullerier's pills.—Take—
Bichloride of Mercury . . . . 1 part,
Wheat Flour . . . . 15 parts,
Powdered Gum . . . . . . 2 „

Distilled water sufficient to make into a mass, of which 2½ grs. to be taken morning and evening.

Dupuytren's pills.—Take—
Bichloride of Mercury . . . 0·18 grains,
Extract of Opium . . . . 0·22 „
Extract of Guaiacum . . . 0·75 „

For one pill, two of which to be taken daily.

Ricord's formula.—Take—

Proto-iodide of Mercury . } *aa* 45 grains,
Extract of Lettuce . . . }
Extract of Opium . . . . . 15 „
Confection of Roses . . . . 90 „

For sixty pills, one, two, or three to be taken daily.

Puche's Syrup.—Take—

Iodo-hydrargyrate of Potash . . 1 part,
Iodine . . . . 1 „
Iodide of Potassium . . . . . 20 parts,
Syrup of Wild Poppies . . . 473 „

This syrup is well suited for persons of lymphatic constitution, who have reached the end of the second stage.

INDEX.

NEW PUBLICATION. Fcap. 8vo., pp. 252, handsomely bound, gilt lettered and side, price 3s. 6d.

ESSENTIALS OF DIET;

OR,

HINTS ON FOOD IN HEALTH AND DISEASE.

By the late Dr. HARRIS RUDDOCK.

Corrected and Revised by E. B. SHULDHAM, M.D., M.R.C.S., M.A. Oxon.

RECENT REVIEWS.

" In homœopathic literature diet has hitherto been considered solely as among the causes of disease, and as presenting antidotes to medicines. So our homœopathic dietaries have been generally a mere list of articles of diet likely to be prejudicial to sick persons, or such as would blunt the sensibility of the system to medicine. We have also a good homœopathic cookery book to aid in the carrying out of these two principles, but little attention has been paid to diet as especially applicable to particular diseases, or even as a means of cure in itself. This book supplies that want, and gives us in a handy form the essentials, as it professes, in these particulars. We cannot say that the theoretical views are quite up to the day, for they savour too much of the chemical theories of physiology, but this is of little importance, as we think the practical directions are extremely well chosen, and, in the main, in accordance with the best authorities on the subject. In fact, this book supplies what, as regards diet, we would be disposed to put into the third section of the therapeutic part of the *Hahnemann Society's Repertory*, if that much-wanted work ever comes to completion. We cannot give it greater praise, and cordially recommend it in the meantime."—*The British Journal of Homœopathy*.

" One last work from the pen of the late Dr. Ruddock, lately published under the editorial care of Dr. Shuldham, will not be found the least useful of the books prepared by that prolific author. It is entitled ' Essentials of Diet; or, Hints on Food in Health and Disease.' The subject has been treated somewhat abundantly of late years, and there is little excuse now for any well-read person to torment his stomach with food not suitable for it. The danger is, that a course of this kind of literature may lead one to torment his imagination with distorted pictures of the frightful effects of almost any meal he may happen to take; and we are inclined to think that dyspepsia is almost as closely dependent on the imagination as on the stomach. Dr. Ruddock's small treatise, like all his works, is simple and practical. It gives no elaborate chemical tables of analyses, nor does the author treat his invalid clients like criminals in a prison, weighing out to them the exact amount of nitrogenous, carbonaceous, and mineral foods which they are to take in each twenty-four hours. Half the book is devoted to a consideration of the qualities of the various kinds of foods, and the rest is occupied with chapters on the diet most desirable in the various disorders resulting from dyspepsia, and under special circumstances. A series of useful recipes is added, which tell how to prepare in the best way any of the ordinary household forms of diet, suitable especially to the sick-room."—*Chemist and Druggist*.

" A melancholy interest attaches to this little volume. It was at the time of its author's death nearly, if not quite, complete, when he was suddenly called away, as, in a prettily-written preface Dr. Shuldham, to enjoy that ' one thing he had ever denied himself, and that was, Rest.

" A successful caterer for the many wants of the sick-room, we doubt if Dr. Ruddock ever more usefully endeavoured to provide for them than in this simple and—because simple—valuable *brochure* before us.

" Some serviceable hints on the regulation of diet are followed by a few pages pointing out the physiological connection between food and its digestion.

" Brief notes on the special properties of the many varieties of animal and vegetable food occupy the next four chapters. The sixth directs attention to the special forms of food most desirable in some of the more prominent morbid conditions. The seventh and concluding chapter enters into details respecting the best methods of preparing food. A large amount of really useful information is contained in Dr. Ruddock's last contribution to popular medical literature, and we feel sure that our readers will find its perusal of service to them in the many dietetic difficulties which surround efficient nursing. Dr. Shuldham has, as we can see, carefully revised the MSS., and done all that could be done to render the book pleasant and easy reading."—*Homœopathic Review*.

" This work, which has been corrected and revised by Dr. Shuldham, will prove valuable to all readers alike, Allopath and Homœopath. The nutritive qualities of every kind of food are commented on, pointing out in clear and intelligible language what is best to partake of, not only in health but in disease. The truth that a stricter attention to diet—what to eat, drink, and avoid—will, to a great extent, dispense with the doctor's visits, is daily becoming more known and appreciated, consequently the value of this comprehensive yet compact diet guide, by an acknowledged authority, cannot easily be overestimated."—*Brighton Times*.

HOMŒOPATHIC PUBLISHING COMPANY, 2, Finsbury Circus, London, E.C.

Seventh Edition. Thirty-eighth Thousand, thoroughly revised, wide margins, price 10s. 6d.; half-bound, suitable for presentation, libraries, medicine chests, &c., 14s. Cheap abridged edition, Fifty-third Thousand, without Clinical Directory, 5s.; superior binding, 7s.

THE HOMŒOPATHIC VADE MECUM
OF
MODERN MEDICINE AND SURGERY.

With a Chapter on Poisons, a Clinical Directory (containing the personal experience of many Physicians), an Appendix of Formulæ, Table of Dilutions of the Remedies prescribed, and copious Index.

NOTICES.

" A work which has been called for so frequently by the public as this, and within so short a time since its original publication, must be possessed of more than ordinary merit. . . . We shall only add that we know of no volume on the subject better calculated to suit the requirements alike of the popular investigator and the professional student than that of Dr. Ruddock."—*Edinburgh Daily Review.*

"Dr. Ruddock has so fully and clearly filled in the design, that his work well deserves the unusual success it has gained."—*Chemist and Druggist.*

" From preface to index it wears the aspect of a text-book, suited alike to the professional student, the clergyman of a parish, and the head of a family."—*Church Standard.*

" Any one who has desires to be acquainted with the homœopathic system of medicine should purchase Dr. Ruddock's *Vade Mecum.* It is deservedly the most popular work of its sort."—*Belfast Weekly Observer.*

Revised Edition. Price 5s.; or interleaved, 6s., post free.

THE CLINICAL DIRECTORY ;
CHAPTERS ON POISONS, Etc.,
Being Parts V. and VI. of the "Text-Book of Modern Medicine and Surgery."
Very convenient as a pocket repertory.

"This repertory is brief, simple, and based on *clinical experience.* Dr. Ruddock is known as a very candid and reliable author."—*The American Homœopathic Observer.*

Crown 8vo., handsomely bound in cloth, gilt lettered, price 1s. 6d.

DOCTOR LOWE'S SACRIFICE ;
OR, THE TRIUMPH OF HOMŒOPATHY.

"'DOCTOR LOWE'S SACRIFICE' is a tale written to set forth the general facts, combat erroneous opinions and prejudices, and controvert objections which are raised against Homœopathy. This sort of thing has generally been done in medical works and pamphlets, but we see no reason why it should be confined to such works. The style is interesting, and may make the mere reader of stories thoughtful. It is, however, just as well to tell would-be readers that the work ' represents in a narrative form the objections to the law of similars, and the manner in which they can be met. It points out the prejudice that exists, and the method by which it may be overcome.' If we drive our friends away from reading it by this candid statement, surely we must be held blameless. Dr. Lowe, the hero, gains a charming wife at the end of the book according to the orthodox fashion, which, perhaps, has something to do with the law of similars after all."—*Public Opinion.*

"This is a capital little story, in which the advantages of the homœopathic system of medical treatment are considerably displayed, to the disadvantage of all other systems. It is in itself a remarkable work, and possibly unique in its method of explaining the scientific mode of treatment of disease. But, though it is admittedly written in advocacy of the special mode of medical treatment, it is nevertheless a most excellent story, most ingeniously worked out, and full of very amusing and interesting incidents."—*Southport News.*

HOMŒOPATHIC PUBLISHING COMPANY, 2 Finsbury Circus, London, E.C.

NOW READY.

TENTH EDITION (130,000 Copies) price, lettered, good binding, toned paper, with a CLINICAL DIRECTORY, price 1s. 6d.; ditto, elegant binding, gilt edged, for Presents, 3s. 6d.; Cheap Edition, without Clinical Directory, &c., 1s. ·

THE STEPPING-STONE TO HOMŒOPATHY AND HEALTH.

Opinions of the Press on previous Editions.

" The present issue is both an enlargement of, and an improvement upon, its predecessor. Its use is not intended to supersede the attendance of the properly qualified practitioner, but only as a guide to the treatment of trifling but painful ailments, or the prevention of more dangerous ones by prescribing precautionary treatment." - *Public Opinion.*
" Contains all that is essential to a domestic work, in an easily accessible form, and in more explicit and satisfactory language to the non-professional than many a larger and more pretentious work." - *United States Medical and Surgical Journal.*
" He who has never opened the book before is able to find the remedy he wants." - *Homœopathic Record.*

Sixth Edition, 26th Thousand, thoroughly revised and improved, with new Sections, toned paper, handsomely bound in patent morocco, bevelled boards, burnished edges, price 5s. Cheap edition, in cloth, 3s. 6d.

By E. H. RUDDOCK, M.D., L.R.C.P., M.R.C.S., L.M. (Lond. and Edin.), &c.

THE LADY'S MANUAL

Of Homœopathic Treatment in the various Derangements incident to her Sex.

" Written in clear language. . . Women's diseases are here treated as clearly as the most exacting student could require." - *Chemist and Druggist.*
" The work of Dr. Ruddock is precisely what every woman needs, and contains information for the want of which she often suffers permanent loss of health. The whole range of functions and diseases incident to women is treated with care and precision." - *New England Medical Gazette.*
" We do not hesitate to say that ' The Lady's Homœopathic Manual ' is the best book of its kind we ever examined. The author knows what to say, how to say it, and how to stop when it is said." - *United States Medical and Surgical Journal.*
" The ' Lady's Manual ' is a work which should be in the hands of every lady in the land. The remedies prescribed are mainly homœopathic and hydropathic, and are extremely judicious. We never examined a medical work which pleased us so well." - *Western Rural.*
" The fact that this is the ' Sixth Edition ' shows the estimate placed upon it by the public, and the estimate is a just one, for the work is in every respect meritorious. As a book to be placed in the hands of married women it stands unrivalled, and yet it is full of just such information as the general practitioner should possess, and will here find easily and quickly. We have seen nothing of the kind that pleases us so well." - *Cincinnati Medical Advance.*

7th Thousand, 12mo., pp. 228, 3s. 6d.

THE DISEASES OF INFANTS AND CHILDREN, and their Homœopathic and General Treatment

By E. H. RUDDOCK, M.D., L.R.C.P., M.R.C.S., L.M. (Lond. and Edin.), &c.

" A very valuable contribution to the pathology and therapy of the diseases of children. It contains for physicians much interesting matter, and also not a little that is new." - *Allgemeine Homœop. Zeitung.*
' Admirable hints on the general management of children, hygienic and medical prescriptions being intended for preventive as well as for curative treatment." - *Public Opinion.*
" The Doctor traverses the entire domain of therapeutics." - *Daily Review.*
" It is a work worthy of commendation, for while written in plain language, so that all may understand its teachings, it preserves a sound pathology and diagnosis throughout, and its treatment, which embraces the ' new remedies ' as well as the old, is in accord with the experience of most practitioners, and is thoroughly safe.
" This volume is in keeping with the handsome style in which other volumes by the same prolific author have been presented." - *Hahnemannian Monthly.*

HOMŒOPATHIC PUBLISHING COMPANY, 2, Finsbury Circus, London, E.C.

Crown 8vo., handsomely bound in half-calf, pp. 840, price 15s.

THE VETERINARY VADE MECUM,

A Manual on the Horse, Cow, Dog, and Sheep; their Diseases, Homœopathic Treatment and General Management.

Edited by R. P. G. LORD, M.R.C.V.S.L.; also by J. RUSH and W. RUSH, Veterinary Surgeons.

REVIEWS.

" There are so many valuable publications on this subject that it seems invidious to draw attention to one particular work, but we can safely say that the work under review is one that every breeder and others having cattle will find of great service. Homœopathy has worked a radical change in the system of treatment of the human body, and in a like manner has a different method of treatment for the animal—a system, we venture to say, more in accord with our humanitarian ideas than the former one. Looking at the subject in an economic point of view, we find homœopathy claims advantages worth recording. Thus the author, Mr. W. C. Lord, veterinary surgeon of the cavalry depôt, Canterbury, when stating his reasons for preferring homœopathy to the old system, says that the remedies act *quicker*, *safer*, and *better* in many ways, particularly in not reducing the strength of an animal after drugging, as is frequently the case under the old system. In reference to colic or gripes, he says:—' The *average* time it takes to cure colic homœopathically (as taken from sixty-four consecutive cases in my official record of treatment) is 77 min., but some cases I have cured in from 10 min. to 14 min. with ten drops of the appropriate remedy. The longest of my cases under treatment was 6½ hours, the shortest 5 minutes.' "—*Melbourne Weekly Times.*

" Lucidly arranged and well treated, sufficient for the guidance of non-medical readers, and not overloaded with technical information : we cordially recommend the book."—*British Journal of Homœopathy.*

"Those who desire to treat the diseases of the horse, cow, dog, and sheep on homœopathic principles cannot have a better manual for their purposes than ' The Veterinary Vade Mecum,' and even those who are inclined to abide by the older fashioned and more generally practised ' heroic' treatment of diseases will find much valuable information in the work. The editors are veterinary surgeons of large experience in the army as well as in country practice, and evidently know their business thoroughly."—*Irish Farmers' Gazette.*

" The section devoted to the consideration of horse ailments appears to have been done with much care. . . . Taken as a whole, this book will be found useful alike in the stable, the kennel, and the cow-shed."—*Homœopathic Review.*

" The authors know their business thoroughly. They treat the various diseases concisely, but completely. We know of no book where we could turn so readily for an exact statement of the symptoms in the several animals which indicate the complaint ; and as far as hygienic treatment is concerned we admit also the usefulness of this volume."—*Chemist and Druggist.*

" The law of similars, *similia similibus curantur*, having been found beneficial to mankind, is to be extended to the diseases of the lower animals. The dumb creation has suffered much in times gone by at the hands of ignorant ' cow-leeches ' and farriers, and though the veterinary surgeon is now no longer a brutal, ignorant practitioner, yet, at times, his treatment is far too heroic. If homœopathy can provide simpler but not less effective means of cure than animals have hitherto been subjected to, we cordially wish it success in the experiment. The present volume describes in a simple manner modern scientific methods of detecting disease and observing symptoms, also the best modes of treating animals in sickness. Special attention has been paid to the disorders of the horse, very full descriptions of their causes, pathology, and symptoms being given, together with the remedies which extensive experience has proved to be most applicable. The administration of remedies is based upon homœopathic principles, and is indicated not only by an acquaintance with those principles, but also by diversified experience in the use of the remedies. The instructions on feeding and housing, and the best course of treatment to aid in restoration to health, are very useful, and hence farmers and others who keep animals may refer to the work with profit."—*Public Opinion.*

HOMŒOPATHIC PUBLISHING COMPANY, 2, Finsbury Circus, London, E.C.

HOMŒOPATHIC MISSIONARY TRACTATES.

Fifth Edition, much improved.

1. **Fallacies and Claims.** Being a word to the world on Homœopathy.
"It is the clearest and most comprehensive little treatise we have in our literature."—*Dr. Hering.*

Fourth Edition, revised and enlarged.

2. **Ministers and Medicine:** An Appeal to Christian Ministers on the subject of Homœopathy. By Rev. THOMAS SIMS, M.A. (late Rector of St. Swithin's-upon-Kingsgate, Winchester), Author of "Letters on the Sacred Writings," &c.

3. **Principles, Practice, and Progress of Homœopathy.** (Fourth Edition.)

4. **The Practical Test of Homœopathy;** or, Cases of Cure by Homœopathic remedies, in the practice of various physicians. (Second Edition.)

5. **Measles; its Complications and Fatality prevented by Homœopathy.** Being contributions from more than twenty medical men. (Second Edition.)

6. **Homœopathy Explained; a Word to the Medical Profession.** By Dr. JOHN WILDE.

7. **Constipation; its origin and Homœopathic Treatment, and the use of Enemeta.** By Dr. JOHN WILDE.

8. **Scarlet Fever:** Being an attempt to point out how the ravages of this very fatal disease may be limited. By Dr. JOHN MAFFEY.

The above Tracts are published at One Penny each, or for enclosure in letters, &c., post free, 25 copies for 15 stamps, 50 for 26 stamps, 100 for 48 stamps.

Catalogues of Homœopathic Publications post free on Application.

A SYSTEM OF SURGERY.

By WILLIAM TOD HELMUTH, M.D., Professor of Surgery in the New York Homœopathic Medical College. Illustrated with 571 Engravings on wood. Price 40s.; superior binding, 45s.

"The author is no mere theoriser, but is well known as a bold, skilful, and successful surgeon, who has made a high mark amongst the best surgeons of the country; and into this book he has put the experience he has gathered within the past twenty years. We are able to assert, from a very careful examination of the work, that as a text-book of surgery, or as a work especially adapted to the requirements of a homœopathic practitioner, it has no superior."—*Hahnemannian Monthly.*

"Perhaps no surgeon's success has reflected more credit upon Homœopathy than that of Prof. Helmuth. Nearly twenty years ago he had felt the want to which we have alluded, and he had barely entered his profession before he made this a subject of special study, and compiled a work on surgery of 650 pages, which was published in 1855. Eighteen years have added greatly alike to his experience, his reputation, and his ability for such a task; and now we have this splendid volume of 1,228 pages from his pen, carefully illustrated in all essential points. The advent of such a volume is indeed an epoch both in surgery and in our school. He has collected, summarized, and condensed the experience of the homœopathic school for more than half a century—from Hahnemann to the present time. In this he has left little to be desired, and has written what no homœopathic physician can afford to be without."—*New England Medical Gazette.*

All British and American Homœopathic Medical Books.

Price Lists on Application. Special terms to Shippers and large buyers.

For further particulars address THE HOMŒOPATHIC PUBLISHING COMPANY, 2, FINSBURY CIRCUS, LONDON, E.C.

NEW WORK ON HOMŒOPATHY.

Just published, crown 8vo., 264 pp., price 3s. 6d.,

THE LIVER,

Historically, Anatomically, Physiologically, Pathologically and Therapeutically considered.

By WILLIAM MORGAN, M.D., Etc.

REVIEWS.

"This work, which treats on perhaps the most prolific source of human suffering, will prove not a little interesting to students of Chemistry, whether followers of the homœopathic or allopathic schools. Not only does every line bear witness to the practical acquaintance the author has with his subject, but it marks him as an anatomist of a very high order. He goes exhaustively into the question of the liver and its ailments; quotes all the diseases, slight or acute, to which it is heir; and describes minutely what, in his opinion, are the most efficacious remedies; comparing the means taken by allopathic as opposed to homœopathic practitioners. Of course, as one of the leading homœopathic physicians, his leanings to the method so forcibly described by the maxim, *similia similibus curantur*, are very plainly marked, but in no passage that we have been able to select do they approach anything like bigotry. The work is forcibly and earnestly written, and were it not for a too free use of technical terms, which render many simple passages somewhat obscure to the superficial reader, it would be found of inestimable service to ninety-nine persons out of every hundred. The perusal of it by a student of surgery or anatomy would inevitably lead to the procuring of some of the other numerous works by the same author. The book is handsomely got up, and well printed on toned paper."

"This volume gives, in a chatty, pleasing style, an outline of the functions of the liver, and of the pathology and treatment of those disorders to which it is most prone. Many persons are painfully conscious of possessing a liver, or at any rate generally trace to some disturbance of its functions the ill-health from which they suffer. Dr. Morgan has, in the pages of his little book, endeavoured to gratify the thirst for knowledge respecting their particular ailments such persons usually evince. So far as the brief examination we have alone been able to give to it enables us to judge, the descriptions of disease are fairly accurate and the treatment which is advised is, under skilful guidance, such as would probably prove useful. One feature in the book is somewhat novel. Dr. Morgan gives an outline, in considering the therapeutics of each disease, of the allopathic treatment ordinarily pursued The book is interesting, and will doubtless be found useful in directing attention to the class of remedies from which the practitioner has to select when prescribing."—*Monthly Homœopathic Review*, July, 1877.

"A carefully written book of over two hundred pages, in which the various disorders of the liver are treated historically, anatomically, chemically, and under other heads. One feature of the book is that a short account of the allopathic treatment is given with each disease."—*Chemist and Druggist*, June, 1877.

"This work, by a local medical gentleman, treats of a very important organ of the human body in a popular form, so that it may be readily understood by the ordinary reader. The history anatomy, chemistry, and treatment of each disease of the liver are here given in a clear and concise form. Although the author is a distinguished member of the Homœopathic School of Medicine, he nevertheless, taking a wide and liberal view of things, appends the allopathic method as well as the homœopathic system of treatment. The work, which is very neatly got up, will thus be found to be of genuine service to those of either school who wish to possess accurate views on one of the most important parts of the human organism."—*Brighton Times*, June 2, 1877.

"This is a philosophical book, based on sound principles, and not at all illiberal. In fact, the book will be alike useful to the orthodox practitioner, to the homœopath, and to the general pathologist. We might suggest that there is an apparent printer's error on the fourteenth page, in which the well-known word 'officinal' has been printed twice over 'official.' This can easily be altered in the second edition, which is sure to be required of this useful and convenient little manual of hepatic diseases."—*Public Opinion*, June 23, 1877.

LONDON:

HOMŒOPATHIC PUBLISHING COMPANY, 2, Finsbury Circus, E.C.

NEW WORK ON HOMŒOPATHY.

Now ready, crown 8vo., 200 pp., price 3s. 6d.,

DIABETES MELLITUS:

Its History, Chemistry, Anatomy, Pathology, Physiology, and Treatment.

Illustrated with Woodcuts and Cases.

By WILLIAM MORGAN, M.D., Etc.

This Work forms an Historic Record of the Pathology and Physiology of Diabetes, from the Era of Hippocrates to the startling discoveries of Claude Bernard. As the edition is a limited one, early orders for copies are requested.

"Dr. Morgan's treatise is philosophical and exhaustive. The author gives a perspicuous and practical exposition of the nature and causes of the complaint, and we hope that a disease which for so many centuries has baffled the skill of the faculty may be alleviated by the application of the rules contained in the complete and systematic work before us. Dr. Morgan points out that since 1848 our knowledge of the whole subject has been revolutionized by the experiments of Claude Bernard, Chauveau, Bence Jones, Harley, and Pavy. His own researches have further revolutionized our ideas."—*Public Opinion*, July 7th, 1877.

Handsomely bound, price 2s. 6d.,

The Signs and Concomitant Symptons of Pregnancy,

Their Pathology and Treatment.

To which is added—A Chapter on Delivery; The Selection of a Nurse; and The Management of the Lying-in Chamber.

Third Edition, Parts I. and II. now ready.

A Manual of Pharmacodynamics.

By Dr. RICHARD HUGHES, L.R.C.P., &c.

Part I. containing the Remedies from Acids to Guaiacum ; Part II. containing the Remedies from Hamamelis to Zincum, may now be obtained from the *Homœopathic Publishing Company*, who have purchased all the above books lying in the printer's hands, consisting of 2,000 copies, which they are prepared to offer on liberal terms.

Price for each Part, in Cloth binding, 7s. 6d. ; Paper Covers, 6s. : or handsomely bound in one volume, 14s. ; and with Clinical Index, 15s. 6d.

Export Orders promptly attended to.

Third Edition, cloth, 1s. 6d.,

THE PHILOSOPHY OF HOMŒOPATHY.

(See Opinions of the Press.)

LONDON:

HOMŒOPATHIC PUBLISHING COMPANY, 2, Finsbury Circus, E.C.

NOW READY, TENTH EDITION.

ONE HUNDRED AND THIRTY THOUSAND COPIES,

IMPROVED AND ENLARGED.

Price, lettered, good binding, toned paper, with a CLINICAL DIRECTORY,
1s. 6d.; ditto, elegant binding, gilt edged, for Presents, 3s. 6d.; Cheap
Edition, without Clinical Directory, etc., 1s.

THE STEPPING-STONE

TO

HOMŒOPATHY & HEALTH.

BY

E. H. RUDDOCK, M.D., L.R.C.P., M.R.C.S., L.M., (Lond. & Edin.)

ETC.

Opinions of the Press on previous Editions.

" The present issue is both an enlargement of and an improvement upon its predecessors.
Its use is not intended to supersede the attendance of the properly qualified practitioner, but
only as a guide to the treatment of trifling but painful ailments, or the prevention of more
dangerous ones, by prescribing precautionary treatment."—*Public Opinion.*

" Contains all that is essential to a domestic work, in an easy accessible form, and in more
explicit and satisfactory language to the non-professional than many a larger and more pretentious work."—*United States Medical and Surgical Journal.*

" He who has never opened the book before is able to find the remedy he wants."—
Homœopathic Record.

" A perfect manual on a vital subject, and a copy should be in every home."—*Wesleyan
Times.*

" *Nolens volens*, we physicians have to give in, for laymen will, without our permission,
try their hand on doctoring; and the best we can do is to instruct them to do it in the right
manner; and, after all, it pays even to the doctors, for there is no better proselyte-maker
than a lay woman who has performed some ' miraculous cure ' with *Aconite* and *Chamomilla.*
May this and similar works be spread broadcast over the land. May they sow the seed, and
the homœopathic fraternity will enjoy the fruit. So may it be! "—*North American
Journal of Homœopathy.*

" The issue of 100,000 (now 130,000) copies of one of Dr. Ruddock's books indicates the
number of those who are inquiring into, if not practising, Homœopathy—for he is not the only
homœopathic writer, although he holds a high place among his compeers. An epitome of
the homœopathic system—exceedingly useful for learners."—From *Dundee Advertiser.*

" This is a very comprehensive manual, on a very interesting subject. They who wish to
obtain a clear bird's-eye view of the system will find the volume reliable."—*British Standard.*

" The volume contains a great amount of information on the symptoms, causes, and treatment of diseases of most frequent occurrence. It also treats of the diet and accessory
measures connected with the practice of domestic Homœopathy."—*Halifax Observer.*

" It is devoid of all medical technicalities, and is written in a style so simple that the most
inexperienced can understand it."—*National Standard.*

" Clever, clear, and simple guide to Homœopathy and Health."—*Weekly Record.*

HOMŒOPATHIC PUBLISHING COMPANY,

2, FINSBURY CIRCUS, LONDON, E.C.

AND ALL HOMŒOPATHIC CHEMISTS AND DRUGGISTS.

Printed in the United States
127629LV00009B/1/A